HANDBOOK OF AMERICAN INDIAN GAMES

ALLAN AND PAULETTE MACFARLAN

Illustrated by Paulette Macfarlan

DOVER PUBLICATIONS, INC., NEW YORK

Published in Canada by General Publishing Company, Ltd., 30
Lesmill Road, Don Mills, Toronto, Ontario.
Published in the United Kingdom by Constable and Company, Ltd.

This Dover edition, first published in 1985, is an unabridged and
corrected republication of the work first published by Association Press,
New York, in 1958 under the title *Book of American Indian Games.*

Manufactured in the United States of America
Dover Publications, Inc., 31 East 2nd Street, Mineola, N.Y. 11501

Library of Congress Cataloging in Publication Data

Macfarlan, Allan A.
   Handbook of American Indian games.

T 5304

   Reprint. Originally published: Book of American Indian games. New
York : Association Press, 1958.
   Includes index.
   1. Indians of North America—Games.   I. Macfarlan, Paulette
Jumeau. II. Title.
E98.G2M25   1985   793'.08997   84-18835
ISBN 0-486-24837-2 (pbk.)

TO MY WIFE

Campwise and trailwise comrade and coauthor and illustrator of this book

Contents

Introduction

BOOK OF AMERICAN INDIAN GAMES has been written because of the great demand from all quarters for a comprehensive book of Indian Games suitable for recreational groups of all sorts, libraries, colleges, schools, teachers' training courses, camps, Boy Scouts, Girl Scouts, Y-Indian Guides, Campfire Girls, and campfire groups, outdoor and indoor play groups, youth leaders and camp counselors, and, last but not least, parents and families who find themselves at a loss for interesting and amusing games which can be played on the spur of the moment and require little or no equipment, and, with the exception of a few Ceremonial Games, even less explanation.

The 150 games of the American Indians detailed in this book should prove comprehensive, interesting, informative, and amusing reading. The first chapter, coupled with the many introductions to games and series of games which open most of the chapters, offers a clear insight into how the Indians of the Americas thought, lived, and played. Neither lengthy nor intricate explanations proved necessary in setting down, from notes gathered over a period of twenty years in Indian territory, these authentic games of the First Americans.

Book of American Indian Games is a varied collection of instructive, amusing, active, quiet, and competitive games and challenges, for both boys and girls of all ages, which require the absolute minimum of simple, easy-to-make equipment. A great number of the games can be played without any equipment whatsoever. The materials needed for making the equipment desirable for some of them can be found as easily around a recreational center or home, with the addition of a little improvisation, as in the woods, fields, and forest. Games of all sorts are included, for all occasions and for all ages. One is surprised by the small quantity of material required to play so many varied games. The details for the play-way of each game and activity are made even plainer by cameo-clear drawings wherever necessary. Practically all of the games given can be played equally well with a few players or by small, medium, or large groups. Many of them can be played indoors as well as outdoors. Most of them tend to encourage thought; train observatory powers; develop patience and a sense of humor, one of God's great gifts to the American Indians; quicken the hands, feet, and eyes; and develop dexterity, strength, endurance, and skills; while other games give actual practice in woodcraft and naturecraft.

It is the author's sincere hope that *Book of American Indian Games* will open up additional recreational territory, Indian Territory, for even the most experienced recreational leaders and the "chiefs" who work with today's bands of "modern Indians."

HANDBOOK OF AMERICAN INDIAN GAMES

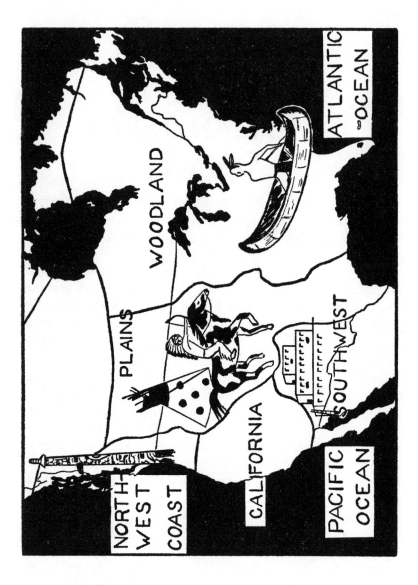

1.

American Indians at Play

INDIAN GAMES frequently reveal the habitat, habits, and principal occupations of the tribes which played them. It is not surprising that hunting was featured in a number of games of the Plains and Woodland tribes; corn, weather, and grain in those of the Southwest; and fishing, salmon, and seal in the games of the fishermen of the Northwest Coast. Indians of all ages loved fun, and in this book their fun games are liberally represented.

CHILDREN'S GAMES

The games played most by Indian children can be divided into well-defined categories. Imitative and dramatic games, often portraying social customs, ceremonies, and hunting; warfare on a free-for-all battle scale; or individual, man-to-man combats—these formed the most distinctive patterns of recreation.

Indian youngsters had neither toyshop nor ten-cent store in which to buy playthings. They had to play with the objects provided by Mother Nature, such as logs, poles, branches, twigs, sticks, bark, leaves, seeds, evergreen cones, vines, grasses, straws, reeds, ferns, corncobs, gourds, fruit pits, berries, rocks, stones, pebbles, shells, animal hides, intestines, and bones, rawhide, feathers, and many other basic materials for playthings provided by nature's bounty. Games were often invented on the spur of the moment, without purchased playthings of any sort to add to the fun. Despite this handicap, if such it can be called, Indian children had just as good a time and played many games just as good as those modern children play, without drawing on a weekly allowance or their parents' purse.

Boys walked on stilts, played Tipcat, and spun homemade tops. Mixed groups of boys and girls played Follow My Leader and Hide and Seek. Battledore and Shuttlecock was a favorite game of old and young in some tribes, as was the game of Quoits. Indian girls were adept at skipping ropes, and both boys and girls played Blind Man's Buff, Tag and Double Tag, games of stealing each other's places, and a number of "ring-around" games. Indian children made Wind Hoops which rolled nicely before a breeze and built bark canoes, dugouts, and rafts which floated well on lakes and streams.

Boys delighted in many sorts of athletic games. They ran races, contested in high and broad jumps as well as hurdle jumping, wrestled, hopped, and played many challenge games, some of which were hand pulling, foot pulling, neck pulling, head pushing, pole pushing and pulling, mimic warfare, taking prisoners, and numerous other games based on hunting and warfare. Indian children, because of their outdoor life and athletic activities, were more mature and stronger for their ages than most modern children. They played many really rough and tough "games," to prove how strong and brave they were. Most of these games, including battering ram, kicking, and grass cuts are ones which should be strictly avoided by modern leaders of games. Another dangerous sport that young men and boys liked to play was racing directly *toward* each other in certain foot races. This was, in fact, a rather typical way of running races, and was favored in many widely separated tribes. A safer form of Indian Foot Race, based on the

Indian head-on race, is given in this book. Older boys played team games resembling shinny, and lacrosse.

The Indian children in those parts of the Americas where each winter brought snow found many snow games to provide exercise and fun. They had snowball fights, built and stormed snow forts, made toboggans from rawhide, strips of wood, and bark. The word *toboggan* is of Algonquin origin. The youngsters also used to play exciting tracking games in the snow, either making trails of their own or following the tracks of many kinds of animals. Their fathers and older brothers played more difficult games, Snow Snake, for example. This game has been so often described in books dealing with American Indian life, and suitable equipment and the play area are so hard to make and lay out, that it will not be dealt with in this book. Instead, another less-known game, called Snow Boat— a game dear to the hearts of the warriors and youngsters of the Six Nations, and especially the Seneca and Iroquois—is described in the chapter on "Skill Games."

JUVENILE IMITATIVE GAMES

Quite frequently the games of Indian youngsters of all ages were copied from or based on the games of their elders. The boys played games which their fathers played, while the girls played many of the games enjoyed by their mothers. The children also liked to imitate the motions of animals, birds, reptiles, and fish; the calls and cries of birds and animals, too, became a part of their mimicry. The spirit of competition was as keen among these young Indians as it is among modern children, so each one tried to be a better imitator than his companions. This trait developed into competitive imitative games. To see some of the best imitators portraying the motions of various birds and beasts is a revelation. So perfect is the mimicry that it is quite easy for one versed in the ways of the wild to distinguish immediately just which bird, beast, or reptile is being created.

Ceremony, ceremonials, and taboos entered into the juvenile versions of games just as it did in the pastimes of grownups. Certain games could only be played at certain times, or seasons, of the year. Indian children liked to be pushed high on a swing. Often the swing "ropes" were made of tough rawhide or tough, woven plant or bark fiber, while the seat was made of a piece of bark, or a skin or blanket folded to assure a soft seat. One drawback about this amusement was that it could only be carried out in the fall—after the leaves had fallen, was the rule of some tribes.

GAMES IN MYTH AND LEGEND

References to many of the games in the following pages frequently occur in the myths, or origin myths, and legends of a great number of tribes. In these tales the culture hero, often a supernatural being in disguise, defeats all human contestants in challenge-games and contests requiring skill, strength, speed, cunning, or magic.

To give one example of the connection between myths and the field of games, the Navaho say that their forefathers were taught to play string games, like Cat's Cradle, by the Spider People, which accounts for the weblike patterns woven. Certain myths and religious beliefs dictated whether men and women, or only men or women, played many of the games. For instance, the women of certain tribes were thought to have been given the gift of the game of Double Ball from the moon. Because of this belief, the game was played, with practically no exception outside of a few California tribes, only by women. Men of the Pueblo People connected the game of Hoop and Javelin with their War Gods and, for that reason, women never played that game in the Southwest. Though varied forms of this game, such as Hoop and Pole and Lance and Pole, were played by many tribes throughout the Americas, it was never played by women of these tribes either.

16

American Indians at Play

EFFECTS OF OMENS, SIGNS, AND DREAMS ON GAMES AND PLAYERS

Practically every Indian nation and tribe from coast to coast believed in various omens, often totally different ones in widely separated sections of the country, foretelling success or failure in tribal games. Such omens were taken so seriously that they could even cause a change of day for long-planned ceremonial games. If the members of some tribes heard the hoot of an owl on the night preceding the games, the games were postponed until a day that was not marred by ill omen. A shooting star, or lightning, seen on the night before a contest was considered a good omen, and the tribes which saw either of these signs felt certain that their players and teams would be favored in the games next day. Personal dreams, or signs actually seen by individual players, deeply affected them and had a good or bad effect on their form, according to the nature of the sign, in the games in which they contested.

LUCK AND CHANCE

Since the Indian tribes throughout the Americas played scores of different games which we would call "games of chance," it is an astounding fact that they neither believed in nor knew anything of luck or chance! The Indians believed that signs of good or ill omen were actually expressions of encouragement or warnings sent directly by one of the supernatural beings who made the path of the Indian smooth or rough, for reasons which he did not understand or, as a rule, try to fathom. Because the Indian felt helped or hindered by the many different supernatural beings who influenced his daily life, he tried to please and appease them with gifts. Sometimes these gifts were small: a few gaily colored beads left in a hole in a rock or tree or some tobacco hidden deep in the forest, where only the being he wished to reward or bribe could find it. At times the gifts were munificent and

17

magnificent: prized ponies, beautiful blankets, wampum or dentalium shells, being among some of the varied gifts given by great and generous chiefs.

This introductory chapter, thus far, has dealt with general background material. Specific introductions and explanations having a more direct bearing on certain games will be found to preface various sections in which the games appear.

How the Games Are Grouped in This Book

The book is divided into eleven chapters of 150 different games, each chapter dealing with a special category of games. Under each game heading, the *areas* in which the game was commonly played are indicated. It is neither helpful nor possible to list the different tribes that played the various games, as quite frequently a number of the games set down were played by eighty or more different tribes. The headings tell whether the game is played by boys or girls, or both (games marked for boys or girls can of course be played by both boys and girls contesting or by mixed teams of boys and girls); the age group which may appreciate the game most; the number of players who can best play the game; whether the game is played by individual players or teams; and whether it is a game suitable for outdoor or indoor play, or both.

Age Groupings

The age range for which a game is most suitable is stated in the heading above each game. The actual ages indicated by the terms used are: *Elementary*—7 to 11 years; *Junior*—12 to 14 years; *Senior*—15 to 18 years.

These ages have been worked out in the field as an approximate scale which can be used for modern players. They would not apply to Indian players, since Indian boys were usually regarded as men when they reached the age of thirteen and girls were young women of the tribes at the same age. On the other hand, so many of the grown-up Indians lacked what today is called sophistication, though they had a full share of wisdom, dignity, and high spirits, coupled with a love of play, that Indians of almost any age would have played and enjoyed the majority of games in this book, provided they had been directed by an alert and capable games leader.

ADAPTATIONS OF ACTUAL INDIAN GAMES

The name of a game directly followed by an asterisk (*) indicates that it is an adaptation of an actual American Indian game, arranged for modern players. The deviation from the actual game has been introduced for the purpose of making certain games safer, less complicated, more amusing for modern players, or better adapted to their play-ways. In most games the suggested adaptation follows the description of how the game was actually played by the Indians.

KEEPING SCORE

The method of keeping score suggested for the various games is the one which proves the simplest and most effective for modern Indian bands. Modern chiefs can use their own scoring methods.

INDIAN TERMINOLOGY

Indian words and phrases have been avoided as much as possible in this book, as their translation into English best serves the purpose. The words *coup* and *grand coup* and to *count coup* have been used at times. They refer—as leaders of modern Indian bands know—to honors and exploits and the winning of challenge-games and challenges, as the Indians used these words to describe war exploits, after adopting them from French pioneers.

BOUNDARY MARKERS AND STAPLES[*]

From time to time throughout this book, markers, and staples to hold them in place, have been mentioned. Definite boundaries and the start and finish points of all games which require them should be plainly indicated. Handy markers can easily be made from strips of stout, tough cardboard, painted yellow or white to assure visibility. These markers can be 12 inches long and 3 inches wide. Markers can also be made from small circles or squares of cardboard, cloth, or even paper. Tough paper plates of various sizes also make good emergency markers.

All markers of the kind mentioned should be securely held in place so that they cannot be dislodged by the running feet of players. Homemade wire staples can speedily be made to hold such markers in place. A piece of strong but pliable wire 10 inches long and about ¼ inch in diameter should be bent in two places toward the middle of the wire in order to make a flat-topped staple with a top of about 3 inches. This will give the staple two legs 3½ inches long. The length of the staple legs is best decided by the hardness or softness of the ground into which they have to be thrust. Prepared holes may be made in plate-markers or strip-markers through which the staple legs pass before being pushed into the ground. These staples are, of course, always pushed down flush onto the marker so that there is absolutely nothing left above ground for the players to trip over.

[*] Adapted from *More New Games for 'Tween-Agers*, Allan A. Macfarlan (New York: Association Press, 1958), pp. 33–36.

2.

Running and Relay Games

KIWA TRAIL*

Northwest Coast—Woodland

BOYS OR GIRLS   4 TO 18 PLAYERS   OUTDOORS
ELEMENTARY—SENIOR   INDIVIDUAL—TEAM   OR INDOORS

A number of games played by the Indian youngsters of the Northwest Coast and Woodland tribes were played by running as swiftly as possible around various lines or patterns of standing trees. Sometimes one player chased another around these obstacles in a sort of tag game, while at other times the object of the game seemed to be for the players to become as dizzy as possible by circling trees growing close together. All such games were dangerous, as all of the versions offered too great a chance of running into a tree at full tilt. This perfectly safe adaptation for modern Indians can still use the Indian name of *Kiwa Trail*, as the trail followed is just as twisted, or crooked, as the one pictured by the Chinook name. Modern chiefs can call the game Twisted Trail. They will find it still presents all of the difficulties and fun of the original game but without any of its risks.

Six round or square cardboard markers about 8 inches in diameter are required for each "trail." Paper plates make good markers for this and similar games. A line is marked on the ground about 30 to 40 feet or more in length. Each trail is laid by placing the first marker 10 feet away from the starting line and the other five in a straight line with it, one long pace apart, say about 4 feet. The desired number of trails are laid out in exactly the same manner with lanes 8 feet in width between the lines. The pattern is completed by marking another long straight line on the ground 10 feet away from the end (the sixth) marker. With everything now ready for play, the name of the game appears to be a misnomer—but wait till it gets cracking!

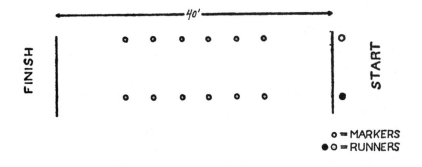

A player lines up just behind the starting line and directly opposite the first marker on the trail. There is one player for each trail. When the chief gives the "Go!" signal, each player must run completely around each marker, keeping as close to it as possible, until he has circled all the markers, always traveling in the same direction, and reached the finish line. The first player to arrive there counts coup and wins. For older players this race can be run in both directions, the winner being decided by the arrival back at the starting line, after having circled each marker on the way back to the starting point also.

As a team relay, Twisted Trail also provides good fun. Teams of from three to six runners line up behind the starting line. On the word "Go!" the first runner starts out and circles all markers until he reaches the finish line. Then, and not before, the second runner goes into action, and the race continues in this way until the last runner on each team has followed the Kiwa Trail to its twisted end. In this relay form, all runners can be asked to race along the trail in both directions, as described in the individual race, before touching off the next runner.

This relay can also be carried out by having teams, with an equal number of runners in each, race half of its number from each end of the trail. In this way, the first runner on the team at the starting line touches off the first runner at the other end of the trail, and so on, until all have taken part.

Additional fun and difficulty can be had by placing the markers closer together and using ten instead of six markers, or having players run twice around each marker, always traveling in the same direction! Runners who take part in any of these versions of this race will find that it is a dizzy event.

FISH TRAP

Northwest Coast

BOYS	8 TO 16 PLAYERS	OUTDOORS
ELEMENTARY—JUNIOR	INDIVIDUAL	

In this game, played by Indian boys of all ages, there were anywhere from four to twelve "fishermen" and one to three "fish." Some groups liked to play this fish-netting game with only one fish to be netted, since they considered it more fun. The fishermen joined hands, the fish was given about a 20-foot start, and the game was on. The fish ran and doubled and dodged in an effort to escape being caught in the trap. This was not as difficult as it seems because the individual fisherman could neither touch nor trip the fish. A catch was made only when the two ends of the trap met, with the fish inside, at which point the fish gave up without any attempt to break out of or dodge under the net.

Though the tough, sure-footed Indian youngsters played this game on almost any sort of terrain that was not actually wooded, a modern chief who directs the game should be very careful that Fish Trap is played only on flat and safe ground, free from stones or branches which can cause nasty falls.

TWIN TAG

Northwest Coast

BOYS	4 TO 20 PLAYERS	OUTDOORS
ELEMENTARY—SENIOR	TEAM	

This rather rugged tag game should be played under the close supervision of a chief on carefully selected, smooth even ground, free from stones. The only equipment required is a number of strips of stout cloth each about 3 inches wide and 50 or 60 inches long. They must be long enough to go twice around the ankles of two players, so that they are fastened side by side, as in a three-legged race. One strip is needed for each two players, as not only the Twin It, but each two players are hobbled in the way described. Some Indian players were doubly leg-bound, being tied together both at the ankle and also just below the knee.

The first pair of taggers can volunteer; after that, the first pair of players tagged become It, or the same Twin Its can be used until three or four pairs of players have been tagged and then the first pair tagged become It and the game continues. Although there are almost certain to be a number of falls, there will be players who develop such skill in three-legged running, when they team up with the right partner, that they make deadly Twin Its and the chief should see that they do not too far outclass the other players. Tagging either one of two players generally counts coup, but a chief may decide that both players of a pair must be tagged in order for the taggers to count coup.

BREATH-HOLD TAG

Northwest Coast

BOYS AND GIRLS	4 TO 12 PLAYERS	OUTDOORS
ELEMENTARY—SENIOR	INDIVIDUAL	

Modern Indians can have fun playing this tag game. All players, including It, must keep repeating *Tillikum* over and over again throughout the entire game, dropping out the instant they have to take a breath. When It is forced to drop out, the chief halts the game in order to choose a new It. Variations can be played by having only It hold his breath or by having all players except It do so.

WIND HOOP

Northwest Coast

GIRLS OR BOYS	2 TO 6 PLAYERS	OUTDOORS
ELEMENTARY—JUNIOR	INDIVIDUAL	

The author watched some older Haida youngsters play this game on a hard, sandy, wind-swept beach on the lonely Queen Charlotte Islands. It was the first time that he had actually seen Wind Hoops of any kind in use, though he had heard of hoops being used by children of Plains and Woodland tribes as playthings, and Wind Hoops as an exciting, no-hands form of the game. It was always played in the same way, with light, round wooden hoops which had a few flat thin reeds or pieces of light bark stuck on three or four places on the *inside* of the hoop rim, so that they would not interfere with the smooth rolling of the hoop.

It should be mentioned here that when there are no hard beaches or smooth open spaces in a park available for hoop rolling, a hoop can become as deadly a plaything as a rubber ball. This occurs when children are allowed to play with balls or hoops on sidewalks with swift-moving traffic only a few feet away on the highway. The natural instinct of a child is to "rescue" a hoop or ball that rolls into the highway, too often with fatal results. Having sounded this warning, let's see how a Wind Hoop can be made from any store-bought or other light, really round hoop. Cut from tough, stiff, medium-weight cardboard or very heavy paper, three strips measuring 4 inches by 2 inches. Stiff, plastic strips are even better. Fasten these strips in three places, equal distances apart, across the inside of the hoop rim, so that an equal-sized piece of this little wind-sail sticks out on each side of the hoop. These sails can be fastened on fairly securely with two good-quality thumbtacks, which make the sails easy to remove and they do not injure the hoop rim. Now roll the hoop slightly forward on smooth ground, with a breeze or light wind directly behind it, and watch the miniature sails drive it along.

Interesting experiments can be made with these Wind Hoops, which are unknown to toy manufacturers. The success of the experimentation can be tested by speed and also long-distance wind-roll hoop contests. Questions arise before, during, and after such contests: Will larger sails drive the hoop faster and farther and, if so, how much farther and faster? Will V-shaped sails, with the point of the V uppermost, square, or oblong sails prove to be the best propeller? What is the most effective size of sail for the different-sized hoops? Modern chiefs will be asked the answers to such interesting queries when conducting a Wind Hoop contest. Store hoops range from 20 to 30 inches in diameter.

The author pleased and astonished the young Indian wind-hoop rollers by attaching a small bell, with a silvery tinkle, to the inside of the rim of a hoop, so that it "made music" whenever it rolled. This bell attachment has not yet been thought of by the many world-wide hoop manufacturers. It is a trick worth trying for all city-park hoop rollers who drive their hoops forward with lusty blows from a stick. Such an appendage may psychologically soften the blow for park-path strollers, lost in thought, when they are brusquely brought back to reality by being suddenly hit by a rapidly rolling hoop, with the panting "driver," hopelessly outrun, in pursuit.

CROSS-COUNTRY RELAY*

Plains—Woodland—Northwest Coast

BOYS OR GIRLS	16 TO 40 PLAYERS	OUTDOORS
ELEMENTARY—SENIOR	TEAM	

The Indian youngsters amused themselves and at the same time hardened their muscles and bodies with a number of relay and obstacle races which covered long distances and were often devised on the spur of the moment. The shout from an older boy of "To the sun shall we race before it leaves us to make place for the moon!" set every boy within hearing off on a wild cross-country race toward the setting sun. Nothing stopped them on their mad dash over rugged country except sheer exhaustion. The boy who ran the farthest and fastest counted coup. When there were no real streams to jump or rivers to ford or swim, these were represented by thin straight saplings placed on the ground with varying distances between them to indicate the width of the stream or river to be crossed. When no real rocks, trees, or hills were found nearby in suitable positions, willing volunteers gladly took their places and remained patiently and proudly in them until the end of the race, all remaining as immobile as the inanimate objects they represented, while being completely circled by the runners.

Here is an exciting "cross-country" relay race, based on ones

27

run by the Indians of the Americas, which modern Indians can contest under the supervision of modern chiefs. Two or more teams of four to eight runners on each can take part in this relay. The river and stream can be marked on the ground either with lime or lengths of rope, whitened so that they are easily visible. Poles or saplings should *never* be used as markers at these jumps because modern Indian runners can easily trip or strain a city-weakened ankle on them. The "trees" and "rocks" are volunteers who can be given the chance to compete in the next relay, and each "mountain" is a bigger, stronger player who does not belong to any team and is therefore neutral, as the rocks and trees should be to assure an impartial race. The mountain stoops in a leapfrog position with his bent back toward the runners and his head *always* facing away from them as they leapfrog over the mountain. This means that if a chief decides to double the fun, excitement, and effort by having the runners make a return run over the same trail back to the starting point, instead of running directly back to their teams, the mountains must turn around quickly so that the returning runners, after circling the trees at the end of the trail, leapfrog over the mountains from the rear also on the return run.

After circling the trees at the end of the course, each runner must return to the starting point to touch off the next member of his team by running on the *left* of his team's line of obstacles as he faces his team, when the race is only run in one direction. This is *most* important, as it makes it impossible for the returning runners on the different teams to collide on their run back to the starting point.

The manner in which this race is carried out is best illustrated by the diagram, as it indicates clearly the position of the trees, stream, river, rocks, and mountains which must be circled or jumped. The three or more teams stand with the runners in Indian file and a space of at least 4 feet between teams. The trees, rocks, and other obstacles are *directly* in line with each team, one complete "set" for each relay team. The various distances between these "objects" are indicated in the diagram. The space between the lanes of obstacles is exactly the same as the space between the relay teams, not less than 4 feet. Whether the obstacles are 20 or 30 feet apart is of little importance compared with the fact that each obstacle must be the same distance apart for each team. The chief will

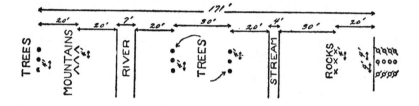

find it easy to control this distance, crosswise, by placing the obstacles for one team in the correct positions, then having the obstacles of the other teams exactly in line with them. In this way no team will have an unfair advantage and no team can say that its members have a greater distance to run than another team. One or two chiefs should station themselves close to the lines of obstacles throughout the race to see that the obstacles hold their correct positions until the race has been run.

Modern chiefs should make the distances to be run between obstacles fit into the amount of flat smooth terrain available for this race, using the measurements in the diagram only as a comparative guide to the spacing between obstacles. While the total distance to be run as shown in the drawing is, approximately, 57 yards one way, a suitable distance for a modern chief, based on space available and the age of his band, may range from 40 to as much as 100 yards. In the latter distance there is little need for the race to be contested in each direction, as suggested above, but an additional line or more of trees or rocks can be added as additional hazards. As only one runner from each team races at the same time and the next runner must never start without being touched off, by a light tap on the shoulder, by the returning runner, there is no danger of collision. To make doubly certain, the chiefs can warn all runners to circle all trees and rocks completely and as closely as possible, without touching any of them except the mountain. It is in each team's interest to do so, as it shortens the distance run by each team member a little. A chief who wishes to add thought, in addition to more fun and difficulty, to this simple relay race can instruct all runners on all teams to circle the first obstacle completely from *right* to *left*, the next one from *left* to *right*, and so on, instead of letting the runners circle the objects in any way they like. This rule, of course, can only apply to circling the trees and rocks. In any form of the race it should be remembered that *all such obstacles* must be circled *completely* and not simply bypassed.

Modern chiefs should make their own rules for judging the winning team in this relay. They will likely differ in order to meet the age group racing. It is not easy to disqualify a team because a younger runner has misjudged his distance and splashed into the stream or river, instead of jumping it cleanly. In such cases it is best to deduct points from a team, or send the runner back to the rock or tree as a forfeit before he continues the race. The stream and river can be made narrower or wider, to meet the capabilities of the age groups competing, but it is usually poor policy to ignore faulty jumps made by team members as, sooner or later, a remark will be heard which intimates that a losing team feels it would have won the race had its members splashed into the river instead of jumping it cleanly.

BALL RELAY

Plains—Northwest Coast

BOYS   8 TO 24 PLAYERS   OUTDOORS
ELEMENTARY—SENIOR   TEAM

The Indians played this dribble ball game with a round bladder taken from an animal or sea mammal. Often the bladder was covered with a closely woven mesh net to protect it against rough usage. Modern Indians can play the same game by using a volleyball or basketball.

A team of four to six players stands with the players in a straight line, all facing in the same direction, and from 15 to 20 feet apart. A line is marked on the ground 10 feet in front of the first player. The other teams line up in the same formation, with a space of 6 feet between teams. A basketball is given to the last player in line on each team.

When the chief says "Go!" each last player dribbles the ball up to the player just ahead of him who, as soon as the ball strikes his leg, dribbles it on to the next player in front of him. Should a player dribble the ball beyond the player to whom he is supposed to dribble it, he must turn and dribble the ball back to the player whose turn it is to advance the ball before that player can take over. The chief who referees the game should see that each player actually *dribbles* the ball from foot to foot, to the player in front of him, and may disqualify a team when one of its members tries to save time by kicking the ball several feet in front of him in one kick. When the first player in the line receives the ball he dribbles it forward to the line directly in front of him, and the first player to reach the line wins for his team. Each player who has dribbled the ball should return to his place in the line after he has passed it on to the player ahead of him. This makes it easy to continue play in the version which follows.

The variation which lengthens the duration of this game and makes the result a little more uncertain is to have the first player, as soon as he has dribbled the ball to the line in front of him, shout "Turn!" and then dribble the ball back to the next player in line. For this version, a line has also to be marked plainly on the ground 6 feet behind the last player on each team before the game starts. In this way, the ball is dribbled up and down the line by each team instead of only up the line. Coup can be counted by the winning team after each single or double dribble, or the chief may decide the winner on the best-out-of-three-tries basis.

STICK RELAY

Plains—Northwest Coast

BOYS	8 TO 24 PLAYERS	OUTDOORS
ELEMENTARY—JUNIOR	TEAM	

This game is played in exactly the same way as Ball Relay, except that the ball is driven with a stout stick instead of the feet. The stick may either be a straight stick about 2 feet long and 1 inch thick or a stick hooked at one end, like the one used in the Indian version of shinny. While how to make the hooked stick is told under the game of shinny, it is hardly worth while to make sticks especially for this game. Just as much fun, perhaps more, can be had by using the straight stick, which makes the game more difficult. The ball must be dribbled with the stick, which means hitting it forward with sharp taps rather than driving it forward as far as possible with each stroke.

The players line up in exactly the same manner as they did for Ball Relay and no player can move forward with the ball, except the last one, of course, until the ball has been driven against his leg by the player behind him; then he drives the ball forward to the next member of his team. The ball must not be touched by hands or feet in this game and the player who does so disqualifies his team.

As in the Ball Relay game, Stick Relay may be played either from one end of the line to the other or may be continued so that the ball travels both up and down the line to complete a game before a team can count coup. The winning team can be decided by the result of each complete game or by the score on a best-out-of-three basis.

DOUBLE RELAY

Plains—Northwest Coast

BOYS	8 TO 24 PLAYERS	✓ OUTDOORS
ELEMENTARY—JUNIOR	TEAM	

This version of the two games which precede it is played with both feet *and* a stick. The ball is first dribbled up the line of players by using the feet. When it has been dribbled up to the line in front of the first player, he dribbles it back with the stick to the next player and the game continues down the line until each player has had a chance to dribble the ball both with his feet and with his stick. Coup can be counted at the end of each double dribble, or the chief can decide that the ball will have to be taken up and down the line twice, by each method and each player, before coup can be counted. As in the two former games, each player must return to his place in the line after each dribble made by him.

LANCEHEAD

Plains

BOYS OR GIRLS	18 PLAYERS	OUTDOORS
JUNIOR—SENIOR	TEAM	

When the Indian boys of the Plains tribes ran a relay race such as Lancehead, they required a long stretch of flat level plain. They had plenty of that in those days! Though each Indian runner on each team covered at least 100 yards, we may have to do with a much shorter distance in these days of restricted spaces. Let us see what can be done with this relay race despite the limited terrain at our disposal, as this race always provides an exciting finish.

To visualize the course, one must think of three straight lines of runners, the runners in each line spaced an equal distance apart. The center line represents the shaft and the two outside lines form the barb of the lancehead. The diagram clearly shows the position of the three lines, each one composed of a team of six runners, though there can be more or fewer runners on each team. Three fairly evenly matched teams of four to six runners in each are chosen by the chief in charge of the event. He stands in a field or on some other flat smooth land surface at the spot shown in the diagram, which forms the point of the lancehead. He gives the runner on each team who will be farthest away from him, a long feather. Each team then walks away from the chief, in Indian file, in three straight lines, a feather bearer leading each team. The center file walks directly away from the chief in a straight line, while the other two files walk at an angle in order to form the outer lines of the lancehead. The runner in each line who is nearest the chief stops at an estimated 25 yards distance from him and the other five runners on each team continue to walk in a straight line until there is an estimated 25 yards between runners on each team. The center line of runners which forms the shaft will appear a little longer than the two outer lines but this only seems so because of the angle of the outer lines. Actually each team runs exactly the same distance. When the three lines have been correctly formed and the runners stand ready to carry the feather back to the chief, in relay race fashion, each team

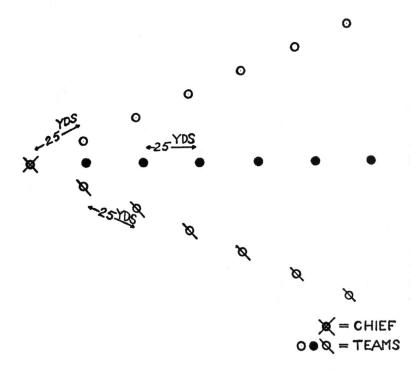

𝕏 = CHIEF

O ● ☖ = TEAMS

should be standing in one of the three straight lines, forming a lancehead, with approximately 25 yards between the runners on each team.

Immediately the chief gives the "Go!" signal, which is best given by one short, sharp whistle blast, the last runner on each team races forward to the runner ahead of him and touches him off by handing him the feather. Each runner waiting for the feather to arrive must remain exactly in place until the feather is handed to him, whereupon he races ahead to pass it on to the next runner on his team. The first team to place the feather in the chief's hand counts coup and wins.

When a larger terrain is available, the chief can have the runners stand farther apart; and when the relay is carried out in a more restricted area the distance must be cut down to meet conditions, or four runners can race on each team, instead of six, which allows each runner to cover a greater distance.

TIPI RACE

Plains

BOYS OR GIRLS	6 TO 18 PLAYERS	OUTDOORS
ELEMENTARY—JUNIOR	TEAM	OR INDOORS

Among the many types of change-places, relays, and variformation races which the Indian children contested, a number were carried out in the circle or tipi formation. A circle was considered a perfect form by the Indians, so modern Indians who take part in this Tipi Race can think of that to add wings to their feet. The diagram shows exactly how the circle is marked on the ground, how the markers are placed, and the position of the individual runners when one side of the tipi contests against the other. If the race is run outdoors, the markers can be 12-inch circles of cardboard, or paper plates, stapled to the ground 4 feet apart. When the runners are in position and the chief gives the word "Go!" the two Number 1 runners race from their markers to the center of the tipi, circle the marker on their own side of the tipi as closely as possible but without touching it, and return on the run to their own marker again. Immediately the Number 1 runner is in place, but *not* before, the second runner takes off, and upon his return to his marker, the third runner runs to and circles the center marker, then returns to his place. The first side to complete the relay correctly counts coup.

Modern chiefs can make this into a regular relay race by stationing two, three, or four runners, in single file relay race positions, at each marker. In order to avoid any chance of

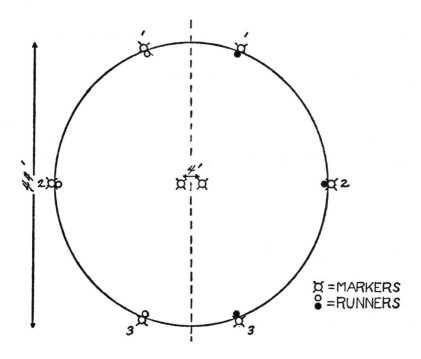

☒ =MARKERS
●○ =RUNNERS

collision, all of the Number 1 runners on both sides of the circle must complete the run around the center marker before the Number 2 runners start, and so on throughout the relay. Of course, in this relay form of the race the first runner standing beside each marker is runner Number 1 and the next runner in line is Number 2, and so on. Or, in an unusual type of relay touch-off, which the author has seen used in similar formations by Indian runners, the Number 1 runners on the two teams, in position at the top of the circle, circle the center markers and return to their places; they are followed instantly by the Number 1 runners stationed at each side of the circle (in the positions shown as Number 2 in the diagram). These two runners are followed by the Number 1 runners stationed at the head of the line of runners in the Number 3 positions. The race continues in this way, the Number 2 runners running, in the above sequence, next. In this way, each runner on each team runs in his turn and the side which finishes the race correctly first counts coup. This form of relay race keeps each runner on his toes, since the runners are not touched off by the teammate ahead of them and none can start until the player whom he must follow has actually returned to his marker. Patience is needed for this form of relay which keeps chiefs on the alert to see that no runners set out ahead of time.

3.

Racing and Kicking Games

TOSS-A-RING RACE

Southwest

GIRLS	2 TO 6 PLAYERS	OUTDOORS
JUNIOR—SENIOR	INDIVIDUAL—TEAM	

Women and girls of some of the Southwest and Mexican Indian tribes were expert at this game, which was frequently a race of several miles in length. The distance was necessary when one knows that many of the women could toss a ring for around 40 yards without difficulty. The ring tossed was a woven ring, usually of strong, twisted fiber, ranging in size from 3 to 5 inches in diameter and about ¾ inch thick. The stick by which it was picked up from the ground and tossed as far as possible was about 29 inches in over-all length. Some tribes used a stick which was curved slightly upward at the thinner, tapered end, while others used a tossing rod 27½ inches long with a bump on the thinner end, as shown in the drawing. Any contestant seen touching a ring with her hand after the race began was disqualified, and getting the ring out of holes, streams, and from under rocks really called for great skill, or an outstretched hand. All of the women in a race used

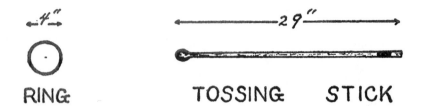

RING   TOSSING   STICK

the same kind of stick, as a general rule, and both sticks did a good job of picking up and throwing the rings.

The race was from a starting point over a course of anywhere from 500 yards to a mile, or considerably more, running either in a more or less straight line across country or in a circle or oval, requiring several laps to complete the distance decided on. This is a good game for modern Indian girls and considerable skill may be developed with a little practice. Teams may also contest this game.

BALL TOSS RACE

Southwest—Plains

GIRLS	2 TO 6 PLAYERS	OUTDOORS
JUNIOR—SENIOR	INDIVIDUAL—TEAM	

This was another keenly contested game for women only. A hair-stuffed, skin-covered ball measuring 2½ inches in diameter was used by practically all tribes that played this game. The tossing stick looked like a long-handled, three-pronged fork, and was 26½ inches in over-all length. The three blunt prongs at the thinner end of the stick were about 2 inches long and they curved slightly upward so that the ball could be scooped up easily as the women raced speedily along, without stopping when they reached the ball.

The race was between two points in a straight line, more or less, or the women raced in a circle or oval, running the

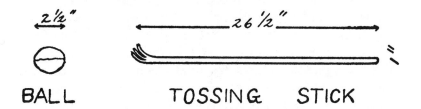

number of laps required to make up the total distance required. The race may have been set for only 500 yards or, much more likely, several miles. This was necessary, as the players tossed the ball with ease for a distance of 60 yards or more. The woman who finished first, without having touched the ball with hands or feet, was declared the winner. This is a good athletic type of game for modern Indian girls and it develops the hand and eye as well as the muscles.

OBSTACLE RACE*
Northwest Coast—Woodland

BOYS	4 TO 20 PLAYERS	OUTDOORS
ELEMENTARY—SENIOR	INDIVIDUAL	

Various forms of obstacle races were contested by the Indian boys whose tribes lived in regions where such natural obstacles as rivers, hills, ravines, big hollow logs, and underbrush barriers were abundant. Such races often covered long distances to test the stamina of the runners. Modern Indians whose habitat is not suited for obstacle races can contest a less strenuous obstacle race course on a piece of flat smooth ground, but an imaginative chief must supply the obstacles in order to provide both fun and difficulties for the runners.

A few of the easily made obstacles can be: a big sheet of strong cloth, or a net, pegged to the ground at the four corners, to represent a river; big sacks, with the bottoms cut out and one side stapled to the ground from the inside, to represent hollow logs, to be crept through; and barrels, after being carefully inspected inside to be certain that they are free from nails and other sharp objects, can take the place of bigger logs; fairly wide planks, set up securely at safe angles, provide hills, which have to be reclimbed when a runner loses balance and has to jump off when part way up. Creeping, wriggling, and rolling over other clearly defined parts of the obstacle course provide hazards which were also thought of by some Indian tribes, and help to slow up even the hardiest contestants. All obstacles devised by modern chiefs should be safe, not elaborate, and, insofar as possible, indestructible.

BEAR RACE

Northwest Coast

BOYS OR GIRLS	3 TO 16 PLAYERS	OUTDOORS
ELEMENTARY—JUNIOR	INDIVIDUAL	OR INDOORS

In this race the Indian youngsters imitated the loose, shuffling gait of a bear while they raced between two points about 60 feet or more apart. Often the chief who acted as judge awarded coup to the boy or girl who imitated the shuffling run of the bear best, instead of to the player who came in first. This was not only to reward the player's nature knowledge but also to teach the players that the correct play-way was even more important than speed. This is how the game was played.

The players lined up just behind one line and facing another line about 60 feet away. When the "Go" signal was given, they instantly placed their hands on the ground and advanced to the finish line as quickly as possible by moving the left hand and right foot forward at the same time, then the right hand and left foot were moved together. This was an amusing game to watch, especially since some of the older players swung their heads from side to side as they walked, in a further imitation of a bear. For older players, the chief sometimes had them turn around at the second line and return to the starting point. He watched keenly to see that both hand and foot touched the ground at each step and that the correct hand and foot moved forward together at the same time.

CRAB RACE

Northwest Coast

BOYS OR GIRLS	3 TO 16 PLAYERS	OUTDOORS
ELEMENTARY—JUNIOR	INDIVIDUAL	OR INDOORS

All Indian children of the tribes of the Northwest Coast knew just how crabs ran. They saw thousands of them, from the tiniest to the great giant crabs which came into the rocky bays and river mouths along the entire coast. Here is how they played this imitative game.

The players lined up 4 feet apart just behind a line marked on the ground. They stood sideways to another line which was drawn on the ground about 40 feet away. When a chief called out "Go!" all of the players dropped quickly onto hands and knees and raced sideways, crab fashion, to the finish line. The first player to arrive at the finish line, who had crawled sideways all of the way, counted coup.

When the bigger children played, the leader might tell them to crawl from the starting line to the second line and then, without stopping or turning around, to crawl right back to the starting line, where the race finished. Sometimes the players who arrived first at the second line were slow in getting back to the starting line, because they could crawl faster with the arm and leg they used while racing to the second line than with the opposite arm and leg they had to use to return to the starting point. That is the reason why the chief did not let them turn around when they reached the second line.

This two-way race always caused fun because the difference in speed of the players always caused some of the slower players to be upset by the faster players who were racing back to the finish line. The bigger players did not mind whether they went around or over the players who got into their way and the players who were bowled over seemed to enjoy the experience.

Leaders who direct this game today with modern Indians should instruct all of their players to go around any other crab met on the way, since the crab who fails to do so will be disqualified.

FROG RACE

Northwest Coast

BOYS OR GIRLS	3 TO 16 PLAYERS	OUTDOORS
ELEMENTARY—JUNIOR	INDIVIDUAL	OR INDOORS

This is another imitative game which amused the young Indians of the rugged Northwest Coast. The chief in charge of the game had the players line up, one pace apart, behind a line marked on the ground. They faced another line marked on the ground about 40 feet away. When the chief shouted "Go!" all of the players squatted down, clasped their fingers around their legs just above the ankles, and hopped in that position to the finish line. Any player who loosened his hand-hold was ruled out of the game. A player was allowed to continue the race if he lost his balance and fell over, as long as he got back onto his feet again without releasing his hand-hold on his legs. The first player to arrive at the finish line counted coup and won.

The Indian players were always glad when the chief had them race to the second line and then turn around and race back to the starting point again. This was good fun for these hardy youngsters, as some of them always managed to bump into slower "frogs" who had not reached the second line by the time the faster frogs had hopped around and set off for the starting point. A bumped frog who lost his balance and fell over was not out of the race so long as he did not loosen his handhold and could roll over onto his feet again, still in the squatting position, and continue the race.

Leaders of today can instruct their players to go around, instead of over, any other players they have to pass en route.

MENOMINI FOOT RACE

Woodland

BOYS	2 TO 6 PLAYERS	OUTDOORS
JUNIOR—SENIOR	INDIVIDUAL	

This most unusual race is actually credited to one tribe— one of the very few activities in this book that are, by the way—but the general classification is Woodland because this was the Menomini habitat where the race was run. One might reasonably expect to find such a race only in the pages of *Alice in Wonderland!* This is how it was contested by runners, usually in pairs, though sometimes four or six runners lined up at the start. In such cases the race was also contested between each pair of runners.

In order that the race might be run in an entirely sportsmanlike manner and without undue advantage being taken by either contestant, the race started about 75 yards distant from the actual starting line so that both runners would, by carefully matching their pace, be sure of reaching the starting point at exactly the same instant. They went even further! In order to assure absolute fairness, the two runners carried a straight twig or stick, about 15 inches long, between them as they ran to the starting line. In this manner, one could tell instantly if he was leading his opponent and immediately correct such unfair advantage. The twig was dropped like a hot cake as

47

soon as the starting line was reached and the two runners raced forward in a desperate effort to be the first to cross the finish line, anywhere from 100 to 500 yards away. This was a much more difficult task than the eminently fair start of the race would lead one to believe because, if the truth be told, from the starting line onward to the finish line, no holds were barred and no scurvy trick too extreme in the wild efforts exerted by the two runners to prevent the other from reaching the finish line first! Tripping, holding, striking, kicking, pushing, shoving, and shouldering were only a few of the many methods used to slow each other down. Braves from the tribe cheered and encouraged the contestants from the side lines, and when eventually one runner was able to stagger over the finish line first, no one could gainsay his right to count coup!

Because of the rather unusual tactics which form the integral part of this race, it is certainly not one to be contested in its original form by even the hardiest of modern Indians.

The race offers considerable scope for a modern "take-off" to be run by two good, husky friends on a field day, after a solemn agreement has been reached regarding the methods of impediment to be used and an equally solemn vow to pull all punches. In such circumstances, after a chief has commented on the absolute fairness of the start and the care of the runners not to take an unfair advantage, this event makes a wonderful "spoof" race, with several false starts to duplicate the fairness shown by the two Indian runners at the start of the race.

INDIAN FOOT RACE

Plains

BOYS OR GIRLS	4 TO 6 PLAYERS	OUTDOORS
JUNIOR—SENIOR	INDIVIDUAL	

This is a different race from that of the white man because many Indian tribes raced so that the runners ran toward each other, instead of racing side by side. Each runner ran the same distance but instead of starting from one mark and finishing at another the required distance away, the runners raced from two marks set opposite each other and met at the finishing line which was marked exactly halfway between the two starting lines. This often resulted in collisions in which runners would be knocked out for a long time. Such races were considered a proof of courage as well as speed, because of the temptation to swerve or reduce speed when close to the finish line rather than face the impact of meeting another runner head on.

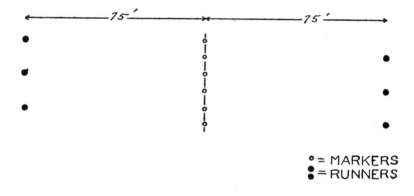

Modern chiefs can carry out a similar race in a perfectly safe manner. This may be done by marking a finish line about 30 feet or more long on the ground and then marking two starting lines on the ground each at the same distance from the finish line. Such lines may be marked at distances ranging from 25 up to 100 yards from the finish mark. Each runner on one starting line should have at least 12 feet between himself and the runner or runners next to him, and the runners on the starting line opposite them should be spaced so that each runner stands directly between the two runners facing him on the opposite starting line. This gives each runner a clearance of 6 feet on either side of him upon arrival at the finish line, provided he runs in a straight line, which all good runners should do in order to assure running the least possible distance.

To make doubly sure that no collisions can occur in the longer races, such as the 100-yard dash, where runners have more chance to go slightly off the straight-line course, a round white marker should be stapled to the ground on the finish line directly in front of each runner in order that he may follow a straight line, making collision impossible.

It may surprise some chiefs to see the difference in time made by some runners in this form of foot race as compared with the time made when the rivals race side by side.

BOY BEAT GIRL?

Southwest

BOYS AND GIRLS	2 TO 8 PLAYERS	OUTDOORS
JUNIOR—SENIOR	INDIVIDUAL	

Often Apache women raced the men of their tribe and won. The event contested was generally not a foot race, however. The woman raced while tossing a double ball ahead of her with a long stick, around 4 feet in length, knobbed at the throwing end, to make picking up the thong or cord that connected the double ball easy. Women of various other tribes tossed a single ball with a throwing stick.

The man raced the woman while kicking a ball ahead of him. These races usually covered from 1 to 5 miles, which is not far, considering the great distances these strong, supple, skillful players threw a single or a double ball and kicked a foot ball. When great interest centered on a game between two outstanding champions, the contest was usually carried out in a circle or oblong about a mile in circumference, laid out in a valley, where the people of the tribe could watch the progress of the players.

A description of the double ball race, the single ball race, and the kickball race and how these balls were used in play is given in this book. The Indian throwing rings, which can be used in a race of this sort by the women, are also dealt with.

The game outline given above may help modern chiefs to think up some interesting and amusing contests of a similar nature in which girls will have a chance to prove their mettle as runners in competition against the boys. It may be that, after a number of contests, many modern chiefs may decide to reverse the title of this game. In order not to lose face with the maidens of the tribes, the author has placed a question mark after the name of this game to show that he is non-partisan.

KICKBALL RACES

These races, in which Indian players or teams kicked a kickball over a course ranging in length from 1 to 25 miles, were very popular with the Indians, especially in the Southwest. The balls, which varied considerably in size and in the manner of their construction, usually ranged from approximately 2½ to 3½ inches in diameter. Some of the Pueblo People preferred larger balls; the Hopi, for instance, used a ball 4½ inches in diameter, made from horsehair and rabbit fur, held together with pitch and covered with buckskin. The Mohave used a ball 2¼ inches in diameter, and the Yuma kickballs were usually 3¼ inches in diameter.

These balls were made from roots of trees and bushes, fiber, woven weeds, whalebone, wood, and—occasionally—stone. The stone ball is not recommended for present-day use, especially by tenderfeet. The Pima, who were among the most expert kickball racers, made their ball from mesquite or paloverde wood, covered with a creosote gum which formed a hard, protective coat when dry. Their ball was 2½ inches in diameter. Among the Pueblo People, particular players used only the hair of fast horses for ball-stuffing, but the fur of almost any rabbit was all right, because desert cottontails were fast runners anyway. Often, the fastest kicking ball racers went even better and secured long hairs from the big toe of a man who was a very fast runner and excelled in these races. Even a few of his precious hairs were worth paying several blankets or mats for, as the runner who bought them knew that his speed would be greatly increased by having these hairs "running" in the ball, alongside the horsehair and rabbit fur inside the buckskin cover. The hairs were always taken from the toe because the player kicked the ball with the toe of the moccasin, or with the bare toes when racing barefoot.

Often the balls were conjured, in a magic ceremony, to "carry their runners along," so that they would not tire during an unbelievably fast, strenuous 20-mile grind. In the circumstances it is not strange that, despite magic ceremonies and the magic properties of the kickball, runners from some tribes wore belts on which deer hooves, beads, or reeds that rattled were hung in order to keep the kickers awake on long race trails.

The various kivas used to compete in such races with one to four players on a side.

With the scarcity of space available in a book, in this era of books, the author's neck is protruding at least a mile when he takes the audacious step of devoting this paragraph to the most astounding fact connected with kickball races. The Pima, mentioned above, who thought nothing of a continuous kickball race of 20 miles, had many runners who kicked the ball *4 miles in one half hour!* The Zuni ran a kickball race of 40 miles in six hours!

KICKBALL RACE
Southwest

BOYS   2 TO 40 PLAYERS   OUTDOORS
ELEMENTARY—SENIOR   INDIVIDUAL—TEAM

Sometimes kickball runners competed as individuals, one against the other, but more frequently they played as teams of two to twenty on each side. Modern players can use any soft or semihard rubber ball measuring from 2½ to 4½ inches in diameter for kickball racing. It is suggested that modern players cut the frequent racing distance of the Southwest tribes—20 miles—down quite a lot. How about a half mile, for a start? Such a race can be contested on smooth flat ground over a 50 or 100 yard circuit; the number of laps decided on in advance will fix the length of the race. The Southwest racers frequently competed in cross-country events, over rough country, but sometimes the races were run over a 3 to 10 mile circuit which had been more or less prepared in advance. A good soccer player can make excellent time in such a race, in addition to getting in some fine practice for that splendid game, as kickball racers frequently saved time by dribbling over terribly bad terrain rather than chancing a series of long kicks, the value of which were generally offset by the rebounds en route. Good kickball players proved that an expert player could run faster while kicking the ball than he could run when not doing so. This is an interesting point for modern Indians to attempt to prove.

KICK STICK RACES

This popular and strenuous game was, perhaps naturally, played by the Indians of the Americas, for all that was required to start a highly competitive game was a suitable billet of wood, which was fashioned and decorated in various ways by the different tribes and owners of the sticks. Each stick had an identifying design painted on it or burned into it, so that it could be identified without difficulty by the owner and judges during or after a race. These identification signs ranged from lines, squares, and circles of various sorts to more elaborate and intricate ownership identification. These kicking sticks were perfectly straight and varied in length and thick-

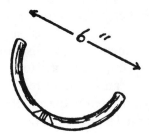

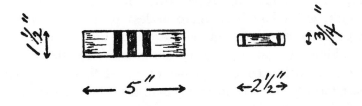

ness from 2½ to 5 inches long with a thickness of ¾ to 1¼ inches. An old Zuni told the writer that his tribe used to use a stick "as long and as thick as a big man's middle finger." Doubtless his memory-estimate was faulty, as his measurement would make the length of the kick stick only about 3¾ inches, and all of the Zuni kicking sticks which the writer has since seen measured from 4½ to 5 inches in length, with an average diameter of about 1 inch.

The Zuni believed that the kicked stick "drew the runner along," so as long as the runner kept the stick traveling ahead of him, all was well. Of course, there was much "magic" in these sticks and an owner would never part with his favorite stick.

As these kick stick races usually covered several miles and were frequently up hill and down dale events, with mean stick traps in the way of fissures and streams to be encountered en route, it is not surprising that the kickers counted on magic to enhance their fortitude. This was desperately needed in the races where sticks could only be touched with the foot, no matter into what stream or hole they fell or under what rock they bounced!

It is strange that the author discovered the most diverting kick stick for present-day use while watching some modern Woodland Indian youngsters play Kick Stick on a Six Nations Reservation. The stick was about 10 inches long and ¾ of an inch thick, but the most striking thing about the stick was that it was *crescent-shaped!* It looked like a quarter moon or a miniature boomerang, and when the youths kicked it, it flew in almost any direction—except the one in which its owner intended it to go! This would have infuriated the expert kick stick racers of the Southwest but it certainly would have provided lots of fun for those onlookers who did not stand to lose a horse or a hogan as a result of the match. I have since used this crescent-shaped kick stick with most entertaining results at many council fires and games rallies. This very modern version of Kick Stick has been given a place in this book for the amusement of modern Indians.

KICK STICK RACE (Zuni)

Southwest

BOYS	3 TO 12 PLAYERS	OUTDOORS
JUNIOR—SENIOR	INDIVIDUAL—TEAM	

Quite often a Zuni Kick Stick Race was an important ceremonial event, started with ceremony and contested with considerable formality. At times the object of the race was to bring rain, in which case the sticks used in the race were buried in a cornfield at the end of the race.

The only thing needed for this race is a billet of hardwood 5 inches long and about ¾ inch in diameter. These sticks are easily made from a length of round dowel stick, which can be bought in the required thickness. A stick is required for each kicker or team of kickers. The race may cover a distance of anywhere from 100 to 500 yards or more, and should, for a start, be contested on smooth flat ground. While many Indian tribes played this game in their bare feet, the author wishes to go on record as not recommending this mode of play for modern, especially tenderfoot, Indians.

The course for the race may be straight or laid out in an oval or circle, indicated by markers wherever necessary. Each player must have his own kicking stick, which should be decorated with painted stripes or designs or burned marks so that the owner and chief can identify the ownership of each kick stick.

The best way to start the race is to lay the sticks out in a straight line about 3 feet apart. A kicker stands behind each stick, facing in the direction in which he will run. When the chief shouts "Go!" each contestant kicks the stick forward, using either foot, on the way to the finish line. Any kicker who touches his stick with his hands is disqualified; and one who kicks another contestant's stick may meet with the same fate, should the chief who is referee so decide. The first kicker to arrive at the winning point is the winner, provided he has obeyed all rules laid down for the race.

Modern kickers who like this form of race can, when they develop the considerable skill required to be fast and sure kick stick runners, race for longer distances and over rougher ground. Such events will be found hard on even soccer boots, however.

These races may be contested as team events, with two to four players on each team kicking one stick. Two players to a team will probably be found the most satisfactory way for modern Indians to contest this event.

KICK STICK*
Woodland

BOYS	3 TO 12 PLAYERS	OUTDOORS
ELEMENTARY—SENIOR	INDIVIDUAL—TEAM	

This is the amusing version of a kick stick race spoken of in the introduction to these races. Much fun can be had from this event whether it is contested around a council fire area, which rarely measures more than about 90 feet in circumference, or in a straight course race of 50 to 100 yards. This distance will be found quite long enough when the erratic actions of the kick stick is considered.

As in the preceding race, a kick stick is required for each player or team. The shape of this circular kick stick is shown in the drawing. It is 10 inches long and about ¾ inch in diameter. It may be made from hardwood or softwood. The curve in the stick can be made by drawing both ends of a green, supple stick of the right size toward each other so that they are about 5 inches apart and tying them in that position until dry, so that the stick retains the curve. A length of green willow will serve the purpose. With a piece of strong string tied onto each end of the straight stick and then tied securely together after the stick has been bent into the right shape, it will make a satisfactory kick stick for this game. The sticks may also be steamed or heat-treated so that they take and retain the curved form. The exact curve is not as important as having the same amount of curve in each contestant's stick. This prevents a kick stick racer with a comparatively straight stick, which performs few antics when kicked, from having a very considerable advantage over an opponent with a correctly curved stick, which does all sorts of unexpected things when it is kicked, especially in the wrong place.

Sticks shaped as in the illustration are the hardest to kick in any given direction and therefore provide the most fun. These sticks may be painted or decorated and some simple part of the decoration should form the stick owner's mark, so that the stick may be easily identified. As in the preceding kick stick race, this one may be contested by either individual kickers or teams of kickers. Two kickers to a team will probably be found the most satisfactory in contesting this race in its team form. When this race is run on a circular course and the stick goes outside the circle, it must be retrieved, by kicking to the point where it went out of the circle, and the race continued from there.

4.

Hunting, Stalking, and Warfare Games

MANY OF THE GAMES of the American Indians were devised to develop the skill and qualities necessary to make a first-rate stalker, hunter, and warrior. Wise chiefs of all tribes throughout the Americas realized that a boy who was going to earn any or all of these tacit ranks must be well trained, while young, in the qualities essential to the chase and warpath. Prime necessities were keen and *quick* eyes, keen and *quick* ears, able to interpret the many and often mysterious woodland noises of the night and day. A keen sense of smell, combined with the ability to distinguish between the many deceptive smells peculiar to field and forest, was still another must for the warrior-to-be. Sure, silent feet in the forest and on the war-trail were necessary. The co-ordination of mind and muscle, which meant the perfect partnership of quick thought and instant deed, was the final test of an alert and seasoned warrior.

Stamina, stability, and strength were also required qualities, but these, in healthy young bodies, were easier to develop than the more technical warrior-needs first detailed.

The Indians realized that a keen eye was not necessarily a quick eye, nor was a keen ear a quick ear, nor a keen nose a discriminating one, until each organ was developed by special training. Often the training was rigid because the skilled instructors who taught and developed these essential skills knew that the successful development of them could easily mean the difference between life and death to the trainees. Detecting a slight noise in the forest was almost useless without the interpretive ability to tell what sort of animal or bird made it. A man-made noise was very often the most deadly noise of all! Was the noise the slight, snapping noise of a dry twig, a dry branch, or undergrowth, the breaking of a heavier branch, or the merest crackle or rustle? When a young brave in training could distinguish between these sounds he was well on the road to know what made them, but there was still an enormous amount of sound-lore to be learned. A splash in a nearby lake or river could be a sound which meant food for the family pot, or the sudden departure of what might have been welcome food, on the hoof, wing, or fin. The vital questions to be answered by the young warrior were: which, what, where, and *why*? Yes, if a wild thing had taken off in sudden alarm, perhaps the most important question of the four was *why*?

Even when a young brave was wise in woodcraft and had reached an advanced state of learning in the ways and sounds of the wild, he was still haunted by the fear of misinterpretation of the sounds he heard. For instance, the gentle splash of a wary painted turtle suddenly leaving a low bank or log for the safety of deep water left a vital question to be resolved. Did the sudden departure of the turtle mean that the almost silent advance of the young warrior who heard it had been detected, or was the turtle alarmed by the advance scout of a war party or a lone warrior on the prowl for scalps? Here again, a wrong interpretation might mean sudden, silent death. It is quite impossible for those city youngsters who take no part in the thrill and adventure of life in field and forest to realize how much of the life of these young Indian hunters and scouts was spent on the alert, and how great was the strain on them mentally as well as physically.

Hunting, Stalking, and Warfare Games

A considerable part of the earlier training of the warriors-and-hunters-to-be was accomplished by means of games, many of which will be found in this chapter.

DANGER SIGNAL!

Plains—Woodland—Northwest Coast

BOYS   5 TO 8 PLAYERS   OUTDOORS
ELEMENTARY—SENIOR   INDIVIDUAL

In this test-game, small bands of young braves and hunters-to-be were taken into fairly dense forest or woods by Indian instructors and chiefs and told to spread out in various directions. They were told to listen for danger signals, such as those given by alarmed birds or beasts, and also the warning whistles which would be given by the instructor and chiefs with the band. On the hoot of an owl, the call of a loon, or the warning bark of a fox or wolf, they were instantly to "freeze" or, if they were in an exposed position when the alarm call sounded, to take the best available cover, provided they felt certain that they could reach it undetected in a matter of seconds. Even then, they were instructed beforehand to use shadows and all possible natural cover, no matter how scant, to hide their movements until they were able to melt into the real cover they had their eyes on. Immediately after each danger signal, whistle, or call, the instructor and chiefs, who also spread out in the area used for the tests and kept cleverly under cover, moved from point to point like shadows in order to discover those who had either failed to reach suitable cover in quick time or believed themselves to be adequately hidden when they were not. A few minutes were allowed between danger signals so that the faults of the young braves in seeking or using cover could be pointed out by the chiefs who kept constantly but silently on the move, in order to spot the boys who failed to take advantage of the best and closest cover.

Sometimes these tests were enlarged by letting the novices pass a given point, traveling in a given direction in Indian file with about 30 feet between boys. The chiefs were on the lookout at different points in order to see which boys took the best and speediest advantage of cover when the danger signals were given.

This training was of such great necessity for these young potential warriors and hunters that it was carried out frequently and for lengthy periods. Wily chiefs posted themselves, in agreement with the other spotters, in such positions of vantage that the boys under observation could be seen from several angles by two spotters, unless they were exceedingly clever at selecting and making use of really all-round protective cover. This was not easy at times on account of the lay of the land and also because all of the calls given were so like those given by the real birds or beasts that they possessed the same ventriloqual qualities, making it almost impossible to tell from which direction the danger signal came. Many a hunter in the making was shamed by having an old chief stand looking at him from the rear from a nearby point, while the boy crouched in what he believed to be good, protective cover, looking out through a screen of dense bushes, or *around* a log, in the opposite direction from the observing chief, hoping to count visual coup by seeing one of the silently stalking chiefs without being seen by him!

Modern chiefs can play this game in a number of ways with the certainty that the modern Indians in their bands will learn a great deal about woodcraft and the delicate art of taking effective cover in the course of these workouts. When there is only one chief available for such exercises, some of the older players can help with the observing.

In this game, as in other games of field and forest that follow, all chiefs and leaders will find it advisable to carry loud, shrill whistles with which to recall modern Indian "strays" from time to time. This precaution should be taken during the game, if necessary, and certainly at the end of all such wide-area games.

PEBBLE PATTERNS

Northwest Coast—Plains—Woodland

BOYS OR GIRLS	3 TO 12 PLAYERS	OUTDOORS
ELEMENTARY—SENIOR	INDIVIDUAL—TEAM	OR INDOORS

Boys like Kipling's Kim were taught to be observant. Indian boys whose lives sometimes depended on their powers of observation were taught not only to notice but to think about the story told by a displaced twig or bent blades of grass slowly rising into their original position after having been trod on very recently. Many of the observation games "played" by older groups of Indian boys required more patience than is usually evidenced by young modern Indians. It is for this reason that the following game, which is a good test of observational powers without being as exacting as some of the others, is set down.

The chief who wishes to stage this game must gather about thirty pebbles of varying sizes, ranging from 1½ inches to ½ inch in diameter and in length from 2 inches to ¾ inch. These pebbles should be of as many different colors and shapes as possible, though it is inevitable that to an untrained observer a number of them will appear to be exactly alike.

The chief has the contestants sit with their backs to him while he arranges, on the ground or on a table, the number and pattern of pebbles which he believes will be best suited for the group in his charge. He lays out a pattern, even or broken, following any one of several charts that he has prepared in advance. The exact place of the bluish, reddish, yellowish, and brownish pebbles and the small and big pebbles are all shown in their correct positions on these charts. He now tells the contestants to turn around and look at the pattern of pebbles he has just made, for about one or two minutes. Then the chief gathers all of the pebbles into one heap and each player tries to arrange the pattern as it was before it was broken up. An easier way for the chief, and one which provides a better test for the players, is for the chief to cover the design with a piece of cloth when the observation period is up and have all of the players mark on a slip of paper, handed to each contestant before the test begins, the pebble pattern just seen. On the slip each contestant notes the approximate sizes and colors of the pebbles used in the design. The patterns can be made quite easy for the first few games and increase in difficulty as the observational skill of the contestants develops.

Naturally every modern chief who reads this book has decided on a far easier way of conducting this contest without a pebble hunt. The "pebbles" are cut out of thick, stout cardboard and colored in the manner each chief thinks best.

In order to develop keener observation, the players who make the best showing at marking the pebble arrangements on their slips of paper can be asked to arrange the pebbles from time to time.

GUARD THE CHIEF*

Woodland—Northwest Coast

BOYS   8 TO 20 PLAYERS   OUTDOORS
JUNIOR—SENIOR   TEAM

This game is based on one of many similar games played in the woods and forest by Indian boys. To provide good training in woodcraft, coupled with fun, it is best carried out in heavily wooded country, so modern chiefs supervising the action should all be armed with good shrill whistles to call in modern Indian stragglers when necessary.

The chief in charge of the operations chooses the chief to be guarded and gives him two to six guards, based on the number of players participating. That chief and his guards should wear blue armbands about 3 inches wide on the left arm. The chief wears a strip of cloth 24 inches long doubled over his belt in back, so that one strip hangs down on each side of the belt.

The chief and his guards are given a ten-minute start and they take off into the woods. The chief in charge explains before they leave that the ten minutes' grace should not be expended by a wild rush into the woods in order to see how much territory they can put between themselves and their pursuers. Much of the period should be spent in making a quick survey of the land in order to see where cover is thickest and to find the area where the band will have the best chance to escape speedy detection and move, under cover, from cover to cover. When ten minutes have elapsed, the chief in charge of the game blows his whistle to warn the chief and his guards that the pursuers are on their way. The job of the pursuers is to locate the band which guards the chief and take the chief prisoner by snatching his strip of cloth. The guards remain close enough to their chief to protect him and throw the pursuers off the track whenever possible and in every possible way, defending him best by hindering the movements of the rival band. A guard, who may be captured by having his armband pulled off, may take the chance of trying to hold a pursuer while the chief moves deeper into the woods. This may prove a worth-while sacrifice, though a guard is lost in the action. The game can last for thirty or forty minutes; if the chief is not captured within that period he and his guards, including those captured while performing their duty, count coup and win.

Modern chiefs may devise various rules to suit the groups taking part. Both guards and pursuers should be warned before the action begins that they must not play too rough while defending or capturing the chief. A rule may be made that guards cannot be captured, though they may be held for a minute or two to hamper their defense activities. A rule can be that the pursuers wear armbands of a different color from the guards, and that they can be captured by the guards snatching their armbands. This is an "even Stephen" sort of way to play, but all rules should be based on the number of guards and pursuers taking part. Chiefs are recommended to play this game in various ways and adopt the one that best suits their groups and the number of players at their disposal.

STALKING

Plains—Southwest—Northwest Coast—Woodland

BOYS	3 TO 14 PLAYERS	OUTDOORS
ELEMENTARY—SENIOR	INDIVIDUAL	

This was a usual form of stalking game, of the "creeping up" variety, used by Indians of the Americas to encourage the art of swift and silent movement and the priceless ability to "freeze" in an instant to avoid detection. The game, except when played by advanced stalkers, was carried out in thickly wooded country or in long grass. Modern Indians may have to be content with a terrain covered as much as possible with bushes or bush clumps and sufficient undergrowth to offer some protection to the stalkers.

The modern leader carries a shrill, far-sounding whistle to recall modern Indian "strays." He stands in a little clearing with the players grouped around him. He closes his eyes and counts slowly up to 40, while the stalkers move off silently in different directions to take up undercover positions in the wooded area. Before leaving, they have been put on their honor not to advance before they hear one blast from the chief's whistle, and were told to freeze at the spot which they have reached immediately upon hearing the whistle. All players should have run at least 20 paces into cover by that time. When they hear the first whistle signal, they freeze instantly, knowing that the chief is trying to spot their positions from his clearing. They know that he will move in a circle not more than 10 feet in diameter, without leaving the clearing. The chief looks keenly around, and any stalker whom he sees and can identify is called by name. That player returns to the clearing, sits quietly down, and is out of the contest. Should the chief see some part of a stalker but not enough to see who the poorly concealed boy is, he calls out a description of the color of clothing seen, the direction in which it is seen, and, whenever possible, some prominent thing near enough to the stalker, such as a fallen log, boulder, or a paper birch, to inform the stalker spoken of that he is the one spotted. He immediately goes to the clearing. It should be a rule that no stalkers advance, even a foot, while the chief is calling out descriptions and no move should be made until the next blasts on the whistle. This accomplishes two things: it teaches a lesson in freezing for a minute or two at a time, so that freezing for longer spells becomes easy; and it does not give stalkers the unfair advantage of creeping up on their chief while his attention is entirely directed elsewhere.

When any stalkers seen have been called in, the chief continues the contest—he blows *two* short blasts on his whistle, closes his eyes and counts silently up to 15. The stalkers have been warned in advance that they will have 15 counts in which to approach as noiselessly as possible, immediately following the two blasts on the whistle. This warning need not be given to more advanced groups of stalkers and they will have no indication of the period during which the chief will stand with his eyes closed. All stalkers seen are called in after the 15 count and again the chief closes his eyes but only counts up to 10 this time, after which he blows his whistle three times, as a stop signal. From this point on, the chief will not blow his whistle but will continue to call in all incautious stalkers detected and identified.

When the stalkers next hear one *long* blast on the whistle, they will instantly stop their advance and stand up in the exact position in which they were when they heard the whistle blast. The stalker who has reached the point closest to the chief without being detected counts coup and wins.

Chiefs who direct this stalking game should point out to their groups that what counts most is being able to cover the greatest distance in the right direction, in complete silence and without being seen. He reminds his modern Indians that when real Indians "played" such a game in enemy territory, where the crackle of a branch or a careless move meant the low hum of a swift, death-dealing arrow, there was no advance notice from the enemy that the careless stalker had betrayed his position.

RATTLER!*

Plains—Woodland—Northwest Coast—Southwest

| BOYS OR GIRLS | 6 TO 9 PLAYERS | OUTDOORS |
| ELEMENTARY—SENIOR | INDIVIDUAL | OR INDOORS |

Rattlesnakes of various kinds were so widely distributed throughout the Americas that it was only natural that Indian children devised games based on outwitting the various species in their tribal habitat, whether they were timber, diamondback, prairie, sidewinder, or red. This is an adaptation of one of the games which best suits modern Indians. The players stand just outside a circle 40 feet in diameter marked on smooth flat ground. Two players stand in the middle of the circle. A chief blindfolds one of them, leaving his ears uncovered. He is the Hunter. The second player is also blindfolded and given a small tin box with a very small pebble in it. For safety's sake, it is important that the box have a tightly fitted cover. The second player, who plays the role of Rattlesnake, is told to rattle his box two or three times, counting quietly to himself up to 10, slowly, between each series of rattles. The

hunter tries to catch the rattler, and the snake should be
warned to move silently, but not too fast, in order to make it
as difficult as possible for the hunter to locate where the sound
comes from, before it sounds in another direction. The most
important instruction of all is given before each game begins:
both contestants must stop *instantly* when the chief shouts
"Stop!" This precaution is to prevent the players from colliding
or running into the circle of spectators.

The chief starts the contest by placing the two players 10
or 12 feet apart and then saying "Begin!" Action follows the
word as the rattler rattles and moves and the hunter listens,
tries to place the position of and catch the snake. When the
game is stopped at any point by the chief for some reason,
he must place the two players near the center of the circle and
the correct distance apart before the hunt recommences. When
the rattler has been caught, one or more times as decided by
the chief, it is only fair that the hunter become the rattler for
the next game. This move also saves valuable time for additional play, as the contestants are told not to remove the blindfolds until the series is finished.

When the players' ears are better developed, the rattler may
be given a small wooden box with a pebble or dried peas
inside it, instead of the more audible tin box equipment. The
chief directing the game should also give the players pointers
in various ruses, such as having the rattler sound off with the
box held out at arm's length, hand close to the ground, or
rattling with the arm so far outstretched compared with the
body position of the snake that he can stand silent and motionless while the hunter gropes in thin air close by and yet far
enough away for the rattler to feel perfectly safe, because he
too can hear what is going on round about him. The chief
should encourage the hunter to use his ears to such good
advantage that he is able to anticipate the position of the snake
following a burst of rattling, should the rattler change his place
not too noiselessly immediately following that move. With

both contestants working cleverly, this game is as interesting as it is amusing to watch, and a round may last several minutes before the rattler is finally captured.

TENDER OF THE FIRE*

Plains—Woodland—Northwest Coast

BOYS OR GIRLS	3 TO 9 PLAYERS	OUTDOORS
ELEMENTARY—JUNIOR	INDIVIDUAL	OR INDOORS

This game, for modern Indians, is a version of one of the many "creep up" training games played by young Indians who were constantly on the alert so that they would not be *It* in real-life creeping up, which could mean a life of captivity with an enemy tribe. Though modern Indians fortunately need to worry less about that, it is still a decided advantage to be constantly on the alert and develop keen ears and careful, quick, silent feet. This contest is one way to develop these qualities.

A chief kneels or squats directly in front of three sticks, each about 12 inches long and 1 inch thick. Strong paper, rolled to represent sticks, can take their place. The ends of the sticks which are nearest to the chief playing the role of Fire Tender are about 1 foot away from his knees. The Wood Gatherers, who are too lazy to gather wood in the forest, stand just outside a circle 30 feet in diameter marked on the ground. The tender of the fire is now blindfolded, with ears uncovered, and crouches with his hands on his knees in the center of the circle waiting for the moment to strike at those who wish to rob him of his faggots. When the contest is ready to start, a second chief who is in charge of the game calls out "Wood Gatherers, we need wood!" and at the same time points to one of the wood gatherers. This is his signal to advance silently and stealthily toward the fire tender in order to try to take any one of the guarded sticks, without being rendered *hors de combat* by being tagged on the hand, arm, or leg by the guardian of the fire. The wood gatherer may use any ruse he likes, except a stick or pole, to secure a faggot. He must not rush the tender of the fire, since the contest is one of stealth matched against keen ears, but he can approach the guardian in any way he pleases or try to distract his attention by any

strategy he can think up, before making the pass for a stick. Only one may be taken at a time and as soon as a wood gatherer has it, he takes it to the chief in charge. That player may, in his turn, try for another faggot later in the contest, if any remain when his chance comes around again.

The tender of the fire should not keep his hands in constant motion over or in the direction of the sticks until he senses that they are in danger. It is good to watch an alert guardian reach out swiftly at just the exact moment in order to strike a crafty wood gatherer whose hand is within an inch of a stick he is reaching for, from just behind the squatting fire tender. The winner is the one who has secured the greatest number of sticks without being touched by the guardian. A modern chief can try out some variations of this contest, such as giving the fire tender four or six sticks to guard or telling the wood gatherers to use the left hand only with which to secure sticks.

MOOSE STALK

Plains—Woodland—Northwest Coast—Southwest

BOYS	2 TO 8 PLAYERS	OUTDOORS
ELEMENTARY—JUNIOR	INDIVIDUAL	OR INDOORS

Young Indians played this game for the purpose of developing silent movement and keen ears. There are a number of ways of playing it but the one which follows will prove the most suitable for modern Indians.

Two contestants wearing sneakers or moccasins, or with bare feet, stand side by side. A chief blindfolds one of them, being careful not to cover the ears, and the contestant who is not blindfolded is then placed about 7 feet in front of the other. The leading player is the Moose and when the chief says "Stalk!" the moose tries to throw off the stalker by noiseless movements, zigzagging, sudden stops, a quick, silent step to one side and then a sudden stop, and other ruses. Before the contest begins, the stalker is warned that he must stop instantly when the chief cries "Stop!" This is to prevent the stalker from bumping into something. The moose always counts coup when he is able to throw the stalker off his track, usually by getting out of earshot of his pursuer by some ruse. The stalker counts coup when he is able to follow the moose at a distance, preferably, of not closer than 6 feet for a period of two or three minutes, as decided by the chief.

Should the moose be unable to shake off an especially good stalker, the chief may allow the contest to continue at a slow trot in an effort to break the tie, provided the stalker, who is really entitled to count coup, is agreeable.

The onlookers will find this contest an amusing one to watch, but the chief must warn them before it starts that they must keep perfectly silent during the stalking periods so that the stalker may not guess from laughs or exclamations how well or badly he is faring.

THERE!

Plains—Woodland—Northwest Coast

BOYS OR GIRLS	3 TO 9 PLAYERS	OUTDOORS
ELEMENTARY—JUNIOR	INDIVIDUAL	OR INDOORS

This game was played by Indians of the Americas, young and old alike. Practice will tend to develop alertness and more acute hearing. The easiest way for modern Indians to play this game follows.

A chief is blindfolded and stands in the middle of a circle 50 feet in diameter plainly marked on the ground. The stalkers stand just outside the circle. A second chief should direct and referee the contest. He points to any stalker at any part of the circle, then raises his arm as a signal to that contestant to approach as close as possible to the blindfolded chief without being heard by him. The object of each stalk is to touch the chief lightly with the tips of the fingers of one hand without being detected beforehand. The stalkers can do their stalking on all fours, on tiptoes, or even in stocking feet, since their success is determined by silence of movement. The stalkers should be warned before the contest starts that they must not rush the blindfolded chief before he has time to say a word, but should approach him at a rather slow, stealthy walk, and try to touch him before he can point and shout "There!"

The blindfolded chief only knows that the stalkers surround him but he does not know where they are stationed, nor can he guess from what direction the individual stalker is creeping up on him. Just as soon as the chief believes that he hears an approaching stalker, he points squarely in the direction from which he hears the sound and cries "There!" Should he point directly at the approaching stalker (who may have stopped in his tracks at the cry of "There!") the chief who is refereeing the contest calls out "Right!" and the stalker who has been detected squats down, motionless and noiseless, at the place where he was heard. The chief in charge then points to another stalker to begin his advance. When the challenge is being contested by younger players who cannot keep either still or quiet once they are spotted, the chief in charge can mark the spot to which they advanced with a cardboard marker and have the player sit down outside of the stalking circle, to make things easier for the blindfolded chief.

This game helps to develop the spirit of fair play, as the squarest players will stop instantly when they believe they are being pointed to, instead of quibbling because the pointing finger was a couple of inches off its mark. The stalker who touches the chief counts coup, but when nobody manages to do so, the stalker who reaches the point closest to the chief is the winner.

BIRD NOTES

Woodland—Northwest Coast

BOYS OR GIRLS   3 TO 12 PLAYERS   OUTDOORS
ELEMENTARY—SENIOR   INDIVIDUAL

As the pointing Indian nature instructor told his little group of bird stalkers, "Bird is there but voice is here!" His gestures clearly indicated that the bird they were silently watching was a ventriloquist, as so many birds are or seem to be.

To test the members of the band which he led as bird spotters, the old chief had them sit in a group while he noiselessly melted away into the deep woods. Another chief remained in charge of the band. After a few minutes the notes of a bird came from somewhere in the forest. The intentional wrong timing between calls told keen ears that the "bird" was human, but the problem of locating from where the call came was quite as difficult as if a real bird called. The group of Indians separated and the players spread out in a circle and advanced toward the spot from which they believed the sounds came. The bird notes were in groups of about five and they were repeated at about one-minute intervals. As soon as the bird seekers separated, each tried to locate the position of the whistler. That was done in the best stalking manner—silent, stealthy advances, taking advantage of all cover available, the stalker always aiming at the point from which he believed he heard the sounds. Immediately a stalker could see the whistler, he sat down in the bushes or took other cover so that he could not easily be seen by the other bird seekers. As an additional precaution, so that he would not reveal the position of the whistler, he faced away from where he saw the whistler. After a period of from five to fifteen minutes, the chief who remained at the starting point of the stalk gave a shrill whistle that could be heard by all of the stalkers. They immediately "froze" in the position in which they were when they heard his whistle. The chief in charge then went from stalker to stalker and each pointed out the whistler or what the stalker considered the closest point to him if he had not actually seen the hidden chief. The Indian who indicated the whistler correctly, at the farthest point from him, counted coup. The second farthest who had correctly spotted the whistler took second place, and the others were graded according to their positions and their beliefs as to where the whistler was concealed.

This stalking game can be played in exactly the same way today in wooded country but one precaution, two are still better, should always be added to safeguard modern Indians who are prone to go astray. The chief who inspects the stalkers' final positions, after they have heard his whistle blast announcing the end of the stalking period, continues to blow his whistle shrilly, at short intervals, to direct any "lost" modern Indians to the leader. The second precaution is for the other chief to blow his whistle too.

KEEN EYE

Plains

BOYS OR GIRLS	3 TO 10 PLAYERS	OUTDOORS
ELEMENTARY—JUNIOR	INDIVIDUAL	

This game can only be played in late summer and fall, when thistledown seeds are ready to take off on their rebirth flight. The author first saw this contest carried out by three Cree Indian girls, near Red Deer, Alberta, one afternoon in the sunny splendor of the Canadian Indian summer. The elder of the three girls carefully plucked a big fluffy thistledown from a tall thistle, almost 5 feet high, and held the down between her thumb and forefinger. Then she raised her hand high in air and, while the three girls stood in line, let the down float away on the wisp of a breeze. The winged seed stood out white as snow against the serene azure sky. Slowly it floated from sight and, one by one, at short intervals, the Indian girls took a pace backward. While it was obvious that a player stepped back immediately she could no longer see the thistledown, the author asked why they contested when, by playing the game many times as they must have done, they must know which of them had the keenest eyesight. With a tolerant little smile the tallest Indian girl explained that they all saw differently, at different times and in various weather conditions, which was why they played often. She then pulled three big thistledowns from the tall stalks and taking a filmy, gleaming strand, discarded, no doubt, by a spider which had used it as a parachute, she lightly harnessed the three airy seeds together, so that they barely touched each other. "We race!" she cried as a sudden light breeze made the scarlet leaves on a nearby maple quiver. She tossed the gauzy downs, which floated as one, up into the breeze. They gave it a start of about 50 feet and then set out to race the airy flier. The downs gathered speed but they hardly floated with more ease than the Indian girls ran, faster and faster, trying to outrun the thistledowns, until they vanished in the distance far across the wide prairie.

The author recommends the first game as an eyesight test, but the thistledown race is not to be recommended unless it can be carried out on a hard sandy beach because it is dangerous to race across even a flat field when the eyes look aloft.

BREATH-HOLDING GAMES

Because a Breath-Holding Game is the next to be described, this seems a suitable place to speak of these games. A great number of Indian children of different tribes, especially those of the ocean-bound Northwest Coast, played a number of breath-holding games. Such games helped to develop their ability to hold their breath for a long time. This helped later on when stalking animals or hunting under water. Games were played to test how long the players could hold their breath while playing with sticks, pebbles, and similar objects. The writer has been amused to see how Indian children made certain that the contestants in such games actually held their breath. A muscular and quite often grubby hand was clamped over a contestant's mouth, while the forefinger and thumb of the other hand firmly pinched the nostrils together. In the circumstances there was no possibility of the contestant taking the slightest breath throughout the game. This breath-stopping method did not seem at all disturbing to the players as they went about the task of arranging sticks or pebbles in certain bundles or patterns, stoically indifferent to the treatment of their breathing apparatus!

In order to see how a more sanitary method of breath control would be accepted by the children of the Northwest Coast, the writer suggested that the ones "whose breath must be stopped" should take a long breath just before starting to contest in such games and then repeat the Chinook word for friend, *Tillikum*, over and over again until there was no breath left to repeat the word even one more time. The idea was enthusiastically seized upon but, unfortunately, these merry Indian youngsters were often forced to quit the contests because they were shaken with violent giggling attacks which disqualified them at once, as the solemn little contest judges decided that it was impossible to tell whether those who giggled were really holding their breath or not. Quite a number of the more stoic players did manage to arrange and rearrange piles of pebbles and short lengths of sticks while repeating over and over again, without a second's hesitation, the word *Tillikum*. This was accepted as a sure means of telling whether a player was inhaling or not, after I pointed out that they could not even take a little breath through their noses while constantly repeating the breath-stopping word.

One of the breath-holding games follows and Breath-Hold Tag will be found in the "Running and Relay Games" chapter.

BREATH-HOLD PEBBLE CONTEST
Northwest Coast

BOYS OR GIRLS	4 TO 12 PLAYERS	OUTDOORS
ELEMENTARY—JUNIOR	INDIVIDUAL	OR INDOORS

Modern Indians can have fun playing this game in the following way. A chief marks two lines on the ground about 3 feet apart. He then places ten roundish pebbles about 3 inches apart on each line. When pebbles are not available, marbles make good substitutes. The player squats between the two lines. When the chief wishes to start the game he says "Ready!" whereupon the contestants take as long a breath as possible. The chief then calls out "Go!" and the players *immediately* begin to repeat *Tillikum* over and over again, commencing at the same moment to move each pebble, one at a time and using only one hand, from one line to another. This is actually an exchange of places of the pebbles opposite each other. When all of the pebbles have changed places, the players start all over again and only stop when they are unable to repeat the play-word. The player who moves the most pebbles correctly while constantly repeating *Tillikum* is the winner.

This game can easily be set up for three or four players contesting at the same time, but one or two chiefs will be kept busy keeping tally on how many pebbles have been moved by each contestant. This is not too difficult to accomplish, as each line counts 10 points, a complete exchange of all marbles on both lines, 20 points, and so on. Players can, of course, be put on their honor to keep their own scores. The pebbles or marbles can be replaced by round or square dowel sticks, each stick cut to about 6 inches in length from dowels measuring ½ inch in diameter. These sticks are placed, ten on each line, so that they radiate outward from each line with one end of each stick just touching the line. Various forms of this game can be devised by chiefs, and it can be played in a square to permit more players to participate at the same time.

DUA!*

Plains

BOYS OR GIRLS	2 TO 12 PLAYERS	OUTDOORS
ELEMENTARY—SENIOR	INDIVIDUAL	OR INDOORS

This breath-holding game comes from the Plains tribes. The Omaha were especially fond of it. They played the game with a long, notched stick or pole, from 6 to 12 feet long. The player who touched the greatest number of notches, while saying *Dua!* at every notch touched, without taking the slightest breath, counted coup and won. The object of this contest was to see which player could hold his breath for the longest period. Since a nimble forefinger traveled as fast as an equally nimble tongue, the *Dua's!* flowed in a fast, uninterrupted stream.

While it is not difficult for modern Indians to find and notch a pole or stick for this game in order to play it as the Indians did, it can also be played by making knots close together, about a half inch apart, on a length of heavy cord and stretching it between two points to keep it taut. When a stick or cord is fairly short, the players simply go from one end of the cord and back again to the starting point as quickly and as many times as possible, while repeating the play-word *Dua!* continuously. The chief who counts the number of notches or knots in advance, and counts so many notches for each trip up and down the stick, will save himself eyestrain and trouble. Boys and girls can contest this game. It adds greatly to the fun to have two sticks or cords prepared in advance so that the contestants can compete simultaneously.

STAR GROUPS
Plains—Woodland

BOYS OR GIRLS	4 TO 10 PLAYERS	OUTDOORS
JUNIOR—SENIOR	INDIVIDUAL	OR INDOORS

Just as the Teton children were given smooth round pebbles for outlining pictures, the youngsters of that tribe and others were given pebbles with which to form Star Groups on the ground. The game is found in this chapter because a knowledge of the positions of the planets, stars, and constellations provided the Indians with the means not only of holding a sure course in the wilds, but also of warning when darkness would gray and fade to give place to morning. Such knowledge was essential to the hunter and warrior.

Modern Indians can form star groups just as the Indians did, under the supervision of a chief who has either some knowledge of astronomy or has a number of clear, correct diagrams of the chief constellations showing the principal stars and star groups as seen at various seasons above their territory. Each contestant is given eight large pebbles of different sizes and eight smaller pebbles, also of varying sizes, with which to form the various star groups. Marbles can be used instead of pebbles but they are not so effective because they are all of the same size, with the exception of the large jumbo ones.

This contest may be carried out in either of two ways. In the first, the chief may ask all of the contestants to form, on the ground, floor, or table, a constellation such as Ursa Major, Ursa Minor—not neglecting the Pole Star, Gemini, Taurus, and Pegasus, constellations suited for winter months' contests. In summer, the choice can be groups such as Corona, Lyra, Libra, Corvus, Leo, and, of course, the principal direction-finding groups. The first contestant to correctly form the group asked for, with pebbles of the most suitable size to illustrate the magnitude of the different stars in the constellation, counts

83

coup and wins. Some easily recognized groups, such as Libra, Corona, and Lyra, illustrated here, lend themselves, as do many others, to the varied-size pebble pictures of the stars.

A second way to contest Star Groups is for the chief in charge of operations to give the contestants five minutes in which to form any constellation they wish. The judging is done on a basis of accuracy in the number of stars shown, correctness of formation, and the comparative magnitude of the stars as illustrated by the pebbles used in the group.

In teaching astronomy to groups of older boys and adults, the author has made effective use of varisized pebbles painted with suitably colored luminous paints: red for Aldebaran, a first-magnitude star in Taurus; a pale-bluish color for Vega, in Lyra; and a silvery hue for most other stars. Using a black cloth background, such star group arrangements are fine as interest-arousers. For really interested groups, a blackboard and a piece of chalk also does a good job.

DARK WALK

Plains—Woodland—Northwest Coast

BOYS   3 TO 12 PLAYERS   OUTDOORS
ELEMENTARY—SENIOR   INDIVIDUAL

Many Indian woodsmen could really find their way in the dark by the use of that intangible thing known as "an instinctive sense of direction." It is a quality which many modern woodsmen flatter themselves they possess, though actually they do not.

The boys of some Indian tribes had that mysterious sixth sense proved, disproved, or developed by the following activity. A chief stood alone on a piece of flat smooth ground some 30 or 40 paces away from a group of Dark Walkers who were in charge of a chief. When the first to take the Dark Walk was asked if he could walk to a given point in a straight line, in the dark, his answer was usually, "I can." Before he was blindfolded he was allowed to directly face the distant chief. When the group chief said "Walk!" the walker set out at a medium pace, neither very fast nor at a run, toward the lone chief who marked the terminal point of the walk. Those remaining in the group stood completely silent, and the waiting chief smiled ironically and made as little noise as a bronze statue. Many a young walker-in-the-dark ended up 40 or 50 paces distant from the chief, and entirely out of line, when he decided that he was as close to his destination as he was likely to get. His surprise and embarrassment on removing the blindfold was marked, and the laughter from the group awaiting the Dark Walk did not help. One would think the next walker should have learned a lesson and would not wander so far astray, but he, not infrequently, ended up behind the point from which he started out! At times, clever walkers took advantage of a slight breeze blowing as a directional help. On the next Dark Walk the chiefs took care that no helpful breeze blew.

When modern Indians compete in this test, the chief who acts as a marker should carry a whistle and blow one blast on it to stop the walker when he is as far away from the mark as the terrain allows. When there is only one chief with a group, he may set up a stick with a white handkerchief on it to mark the finishing point of the walk. The chief should be very careful to blow his whistle to stop the walker at a safe distance from the stick or pole, should the contestant on the Dark Walk have traveled in a straight enough line to merit this necessary precaution.

When there are a large number of dark walkers, this activity can be speeded up considerably by having the returning walker return to the group by a round-about route, so that the second walker may be started out at the moment the first walker begins his return. Two blindfolds will be needed when Dark Walk is carried out in this way. Alert chiefs will take the wise precaution of placing small pads of sterile cotton, or cotton wool, over the eyes of each contestant before applying the blindfold. Modern Redmen and pink eye are a poor combination!

TRACKS*

Plains—Woodland—Northwest Coast

BOYS	4 TO 12 PLAYERS	OUTDOORS
JUNIOR—SENIOR	INDIVIDUAL	OR INDOORS

Indian boys learned the art of hunting early and it was important for them to be able to recognize at a glance the tracks of various common animals. In those days it was easy for an Indian instructor in the art of tracking and hunting to take a small group of hunters-to-be out and, perhaps within a radius of 10 miles, show them practically all of the tracks

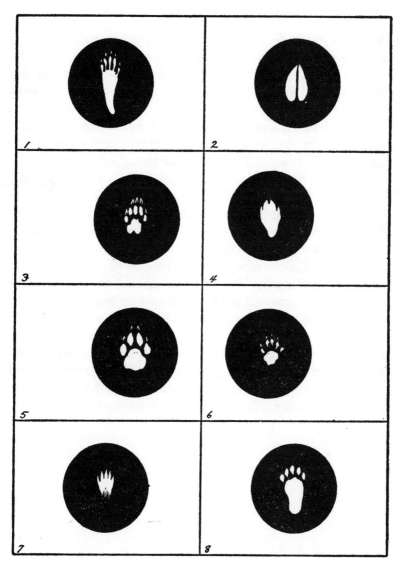

THE TRACKS SHOWN ARE IDENTIFIABLE AS:

1 Squirrel   5 Wolf
2 Deer   6 Raccoon
3 Skunk   7 Muskrat
4 Rabbit   8 Bear

illustrated in the drawing. Chiefs and instructors also outlined on the ground the prints left by various animals and birds in their territory. Sometimes these tracks were outlined on the sand, earth, or snow, or even painted on a piece of tanned deerskin.

For modern Indians, lessons in tracking can be given in a similar way by a chief drawing or cutting out the outlines of various tracks from a sheet of rather thin cardboard. One by one, they are held up for the modern Indians to identify and write down the name of the animal they think would leave these tracks. A number under each track, as in the drawings, allows the contestants to easily identify each spoor. Similar tracks can be made for birds and the species identified from their tracks. Chiefs who do not excel in sketching can use prepared stencils when drawing the outlines on a blackboard. It is surprising how well the forms of various tracks will remain in a young tracker's mind, once he has drawn the tracks accurately a number of times. Advanced tracking lessons can include the tracks of animals that often leave tail marks and the tracks of all four feet of animals that leave strange track patterns. Many young, modern Indians cannot tell in which way a rabbit is traveling by looking at its tracks in the snow.

CAPTIVE OF WAR

Northwest Coast

BOYS OR GIRLS	8 TO 30 PLAYERS	OUTDOORS
ELEMENTARY—JUNIOR	TEAM	

The Salish youngsters played this fast-moving game with two teams of equal size. Each team numbered from four to fifteen players and stood just behind a straight line marked on the ground, facing the rival team, 60 feet away and directly opposite. A chief stood halfway between the two lines of players. When he clapped his hands together, the game began. The object of the game was for any player of either side to touch a hand of any player on the opposing team and dodge back safely to the safety zone, immediately behind his own line. He was free to go forward and touch any opponent's hand, and nothing appeared to happen to the player whose hand was touched, but the player who touched it had to race and twist immediately in an effort to get back to his line without being caught by anyone on the rival team. Any player who was caught was taken by the player who caught him to behind the rival team's line. Once there, he was a prisoner and could neither escape nor be released. The game continued until all of the players on one side were captured. Sometimes this took several hours.

American Indian children played all day long, through sun-filled, fun-filled days, with just enough time out to snatch a hasty meal from the family cook-pot and an hour or two for hard lessons on subjects which would serve them well when they grew up. We cannot begrudge them these carefree days, because they grew up so very soon. In many tribes a girl was a woman at thirteen and a boy a man at about the same age, accepting the work and responsibilities of the family and tribe from then on.

This explanation is given to account for the long duration

of games such as the one just set down. If Captive of War takes too long a time to play to the last captive, the modern chief can stop the game at any time and decide on the winning team by counting the number of captives taken up to that point.

BUFFALO CORRAL
Plains

BOYS	7 PLAYERS	OUTDOORS
ELEMENTARY—SENIOR	INDIVIDUAL	

All sorts of foot races and nearly all forms of running games were enjoyed by all ages of Plains Indians. When a running game offered excitement and skill in dodging as well as speed it was regarded as a gift from *Wakonda* and was played eagerly by the young warriors. Buffalo Corral was a racing game of this sort. It was played in various ways by different tribes. Sometimes it was called Buffalo Pound or Buffalo Hunt. The method of play described here is one which required some skill, self-control, patience, and speed on the part of both the "buffalo" and the hunters. It was a game that gave the onlookers pleasure too, as they watched the skillful tactics and the graceful action of the swift-moving players. This is how that form of the game was played.

Boundaries were first decided on by the chiefs who directed and refereed the contest. These boundaries marked off an area about 500 yards square. Once established, the boundaries were strictly observed and any player who ran outside of them was ruled out of the hunt. A buffalo pound, which was the Indian type of corral, was then plainly marked on the ground in the middle of the hunt terrain. This corral was about 20 feet square with an opening from 6 to 8 feet wide directly in the middle of one side of it. The corral entrance was marked by two posts driven into the ground, either 6 or 8 feet apart, as decided by the chiefs.

A very fast runner who was also a tricky dodger with fine staying power took the part of the buffalo. Six hunters, speedy runners and well-versed in the tactics of hunted buffalo, were stationed just outside the northern boundary of the hunt area. When the buffalo had run out onto the terrain assigned for the hunt, the chief in charge raised his arm. The chase was on! The difficult work of the hunters was to round up the buffalo and drive him, through the opening, into the corral. This was a hard enough task with a speedy buffalo, and they were always fast—the chiefs saw to that—but an even greater difficulty had to be surmounted by the hunters. They must not touch the buffalo nor be touched by him!

Such a chase, carried out by Indian youths, must be seen to be believed. There was no question of tagging or being tagged. If the buffalo was forced by speed and circumstances to run into a hunter, that hunter was ruled out of the game and the buffalo lost 2 or more tally points. The hunters, by the rules of the chase, could only drive the buffalo forward in the direction of the corral provided there was a hunter on each side of the bison, within 10 feet of him, and another hunter directly behind the bison, at a distance of 6 or 10 feet. If there were more hunters in these strategic positions, so much the better for the hunters' chances of success, but even with only three hunters hazing him from such favorable positions, the buffalo was at a great disadvantage. While a hunter would invariably give ground if charged by the buffalo, swift hunters fitted into the hunt pattern so that the buffalo gained little by its charge. The best move on the part of the bison to escape from this cornered position was a sudden burst of speed, coupled with well-timed dodging, which would carry him at least 20 feet ahead of the hunters, so that he could change his course in the most favorable direction to assure at least temporary escape from the hunters. Of course other hunters might be trying to slow the buffalo's rush, by heading him off and coming up on his flanks and rear, but that was to be expected by the quarry. It was at such moments of top speed on the part of all players that collisions occurred and the hunters who touched or were touched by the buffalo were ruled out of the hunt by the chief who acted as referee.

The strict rules of the chase and the efforts exerted by both buffalo and hunters to avoid the slightest contact with each other, even though running at top speed, developed skill and strategy to a very high degree. To watch six skillful hunters round up and speedily drive a not too skilled buffalo into the corral was a thrilling sight. The tactics, skill, and complete co-ordination of the hunters told the spectators well in advance of the corralling that the buffalo had little if any chance. On the other hand, when a speedy, skillful buffalo was the quarry, the hunters had an almost impossible task in driving him into the pound. He used strategies to trick, deceive, and separate the hunters which frequently made an attempt to drive him corralward a hopeless task. Such a buffalo also had a staying power that provided bursts of speed whenever necessary to far outstrip his pursuers.

Modern chiefs who stage this skill-game can experiment in various ways to assure the best and most exciting hunt for their young hunters. Safe, flat terrain should, of course, be chosen for the hunt and the size of it can be decreased to meet the size, speed, and staying power of the players. The size of the entrance into the corral can also be increased, when necessary, in order to offer inexperienced hunters a greater chance of success. More or fewer hunters can be assigned to the hunt, until the game becomes splendidly adapted to the groups carrying out the chase. The top score for a buffalo who has no fouls against him on account of collisions and who cannot be corralled is 20 points. Good hunting!

WOLF CHASE

Plains

BOYS	5 TO 20 PLAYERS	OUTDOORS
ELEMENTARY—SENIOR	INDIVIDUAL	

This was a swift, exciting hunting game played by young braves to increase their speed, develop staying power, and enhance their skill in dodging. The rules of the game were based on the principles by which the wily wolves were able to run down a deer or jack rabbit with the least possible effort and, at the same time, have a ringside seat for most of the time that the hunt was in progress. Naturally the wolves formed a much tighter circle around their quarry than the players of this game need do. Here is how the chase is carried out.

The boy chosen as the "deer" or "jack rabbit" is an older player with skill in running and dodging and, above all, endurance. The other four to twenty players take up their places in a circle, ranging from 40 to 100 yards in circumference, so that there is the same distance between players. This means that in a 100-yard circle four players are 25 yards apart, while eight players would be only 12½ yards apart. The deer or jack rabbit starts to run at any point within the circle opposite a player who represents a "wolf." The rabbit runs in a clockwise direction around the circle, always keeping a distance of 6 to 8 feet only from the edge of the circle. Immediately the rabbit starts to run, the wolf nearest to him takes up the chase and follows close behind him, trying to strike his quarry on the left shoulder whenever he gets within reach. When the pursuing wolf feels tired at any point of the circle, he simply waits until he is almost abreast one of the other wolves in the circle, then gives a short howl and takes the place of the wolf nearest him. In this way, while the tired wolf rests, the other wolf takes up the chase. One thing in favor of the deer or rabbit is that if he dodges so cleverly, which generally means unexpectedly, that the pursuing wolf passes him without being able to stop, that wolf drops out of the circle and there is one less pursuer. In this case the wolf nearest to the rabbit takes up the chase, and the pursuit, clockwise, around the circle continues.

This was a hard game for the pursued, except when younger players chased an older and faster player with good staying power, but in any case the players learned something about the wiles of the wild things.

The fact should not be overlooked that an Indian boy was often a seasoned hunter when he was fourteen and thought nothing of loping and running for 5 miles or more when the need arose.

Modern chiefs can modify Wolf Chase so that it meets the needs of their particular group.

HARPOON CHIEF*

Northwest Coast

BOYS	3 TO 12 PLAYERS	OUTDOORS
JUNIOR—SENIOR	INDIVIDUAL—TEAM	

This was a favorite challenge of some of the Northwest Coast Indian tribes and one which should be played by modern Indians with caution, and only under the supervision of a chief. The same caution is advised even in this adaptation of the game.

The only equipment needed is an improvised harpoon, which can be made in this way. An 8-foot length of wild cherry or gray birch sapling measuring from 1 to 1½ inches at the butt end and tapering to about ½ or ¾ inch at the thin end is all that is required. The heavy striking end should be rounded and the entire harpoon smoothed with sandpaper, so that it is free from splinters. When the harpoon is finished, it should have a nice feel of balance when held above the head in the right hand, in throwing position. It may be oiled, painted, or otherwise decorated but must have no feathers or other trailing decorations attached to the shaft at any point, as they can interfere with the straight flight of the harpoon. Though this modern version of a harpoon is very different from the great 14-foot, yew-shafted, whale-hunting harpoon of the Nootka, it is nevertheless one that can be thrown with fair accuracy and for a considerable distance, especially with some practice.

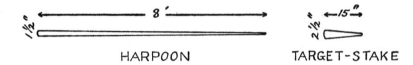

HARPOON   TARGET-STAKE

The best and safest target is a strong stake, 15 inches long, 2½ inches wide at the top and tapering to 1 inch at the foot. This stake should be driven 10 or 11 inches into the earth, to prevent any chance of it flying from the ground when forcibly struck with a harpoon. The chief should allow nobody to stand close to the target end of the throwing area, except a chief or older thrower who stands well to one side of the target in order to return the thrown harpoons speedily. The throwing distance can be 20 feet for a start, gradually doubling in distance as the throwers develop skill and knack. Teams of two to six players can contest this challenge, the winning team being the one which first scores 6 or 10 direct hits on the stake.

GOING ON A HUNT

Plains

BOYS AND GIRLS   6 TO 30 PLAYERS   OUTDOORS
ELEMENTARY—JUNIOR   PARTNERS

This game was a favorite of the boys and girls of the Omaha. Sometimes it was called Pony Game and, like most Indian games, was played in somewhat different ways by various tribes. It was another game in which the youngsters imitated the grownups.

A complete game was played in this way. A group of boys cleared a circular space in the brush or long grass, often fairly close to a stream. A group of girls then came along carrying tipi covers, tipi poles, and other things needed in setting up a village. When the girls had the village completed, sometimes with the help of the boys, all of the players were told by an older boy, who had been chosen as chief, that they must strike camp at once and leave for another site where hunting was better.

Then the fun began! Though the boys did not as a rule help the girls to strike camp, once it was struck they became ponies —some wild, some tame, according to each player's character. The "women" of the tribe had an awful time lashing the tipi poles and covers and other equipment onto the backs of the "ponies." Some of the girls made *travois* from two tipi poles, lashed together about 2 feet from the ends of the thinner ends of the poles. These two ends went over a boy's shoulders, one on each side of his neck, and were tightly fastened with leather thongs over the top of each shoulder and around under the armpits. The other two ends trailed, about 3 feet apart on the ground. Blankets, tipi covers, and other poles were fastened across and onto the framework of the *travois*. While this equipment was being loaded, most of the ponies gave the girls plenty of trouble, shaking off their loads and sometimes stam-

96

peding until cornered and held firmly by several girls until the packs were securely lashed on again. Then the entire group set out for the new village site, the girls leading the ponies by a thong.

The ponies continued to make trouble now and then, especially when fording a stream. Once the new camp site was reached, the girls either unloaded the ponies, not without fresh difficulties, and set up camp again or unloaded the ponies and returned directly to the real village. Sometimes the ponies were kept loaded until the return. The game often occupied several hours, after which the happy band of players returned home just before nightfall.

This game was played so often and so realistically that when many, many snows had come and gone and the girls and boys who had played the Pony Game were old women and men, one could hear an old woman, with the light of long-ago stars glowing in her keen old eyes, say to her companion as a distinguished old warrior rode past in full regalia, "He was a very bad pony!"

FISHING*
Northwest Coast

BOYS   2 TO 6 PLAYERS   OUTDOORS
JUNIOR—SENIOR   INDIVIDUAL

This was a game played only by Indian boys who were good swimmers and perfectly at home in deep, swift, rough water. Not only was it played by young warriors of the Northwest Coast but also by the far-distant Guiana Indian boys.

One player was the "fisherman" and he threw one lightly weighted end of a long woven rope into clear, deep water. Then the players who were the "fish" dived or jumped into the water, each trying to be the first to put the very end of the rope into his mouth and be "played," like a big fish, to the surface by the fisherman. The strong teeth of the Indian boys did not suffer in any way in the process. Some fish not only succeeded in giving the fisherman a very hard time in getting them to the surface and close enough to the bank to be considered as landed, but even managed either to pull the fisherman into the water or jerk the line from his hand and escape.

Fishing, even this adaptation, is not recommended for modern Indians unless played under close and expert adult supervision, in a clear, smooth lake or pool. In such cases the fish catches the very end of a 30-foot length of rope, at least ½ inch in diameter, with his left hand only, and is landed in this manner.

TRAIL OF SILENCE*

Woodland—Plains—Northwest Coast

BOYS	3 TO 8 PLAYERS	OUTDOORS
ELEMENTARY—SENIOR	INDIVIDUAL	

When Indian instructors took groups of young Indian boys into the forest to train and test them in the art of silent movement, "freezing," and the technique of taking instant and effective cover, they worked in country which the average camp provides today or which a modern chief can discover on a hike in the country. All that is needed to contest Trail of Silence is a piece of wooded terrain about 30 yards square, or even less will do if civilization has shrunk such areas to an almost negligible minimum. A stretch of suitable land about 60 feet long and 30 feet wide is selected by the chief. There should be bushes along the trail to be traveled, and branches lying on the ground. The trail can be marked by hanging two pieces of light-colored cloth or handkerchiefs on trees or tall bushes about 60 feet apart, to indicate clearly the beginning and end of the Trail of Silence. Additional hazards to silence can be added when the tract is rather grassy in spots by placing more light dry twigs and thin branches on the trail to be used in the contest. In the fall and winter seasons, dry leaves are excellent to provide that extra rustle and crackle which proves hard for the wariest woodsman, and even wild things, to overcome.

The chief who scores each silent stalk, which the stalker is told to make in an upright or semi-upright position, *not* by crawling or wriggling, can station himself halfway between the start and finish points and close to the trail to be followed by the contestants. From this position of vantage the chief can make notes of each time he hears a sound made by a contestant who is traversing the selected terrain. A chief who wishes to be thorough and absolutely fair can, in his hurried notes, distinguish between the noises made by branches snapping, a trip over a branch, a too-heavy footstep, and the rustle and crackle of dry leaves. Such a complete record will greatly help in the scoring, since the snapping of twigs and branches should rate very low points, while the rustlings and cracklings of dead leaves and the swish of dry grass merit higher points, based on the near inaudibility of such sounds. Another way for a chief to score is for him to wear a blindfold and make a mark on a score pad which designates each sound heard. A zero for a snapping branch, an x or x-plus for a snapping twig, and so on will be found a speedy and suitable scoring method. After each stalker covers the trail, snapped branches can be removed and replaced with similar branches, so that each contestant will traverse a trail beset with equal hazards.

A few rules should be set by the chief before the test begins. For instance, no contestant is allowed to pick up or set aside branches with his hands; or, he may be allowed, even encouraged, to do so if he believes that his progress will be quieter by so doing. When the ground is dry and reasonably clean, a second test may be given with the contestants moving on hands and knees only, or wriggling on their stomachs only, in order to learn something of forestcraft at first hand. The best woodsmen among the Indians did not regard either of the last two modes of progression favorably, for the scout who advanced in this way was too out of touch with what was going on around him. For this reason, except in very special circumstances, the forest and woodland Indians did their stalking and enemy evasion in an almost erect, or in a slightly stooped position, taking the utmost advantage of every tree, bush, shadow, and other piece of cover encountered en route.

COUP!

Plains

BOYS	4 TO 20 PLAYERS	OUTDOORS
JUNIOR—SENIOR	INDIVIDUAL	

The Indian youngsters thought of hunting bison, deer, and mountain lion in their sleep. They learned to move fast and far so that when they were old enough to really hunt they would be able to take care of themselves when the chase was on. Here is one of the many games they played in order to develop swiftness of foot and hand, and the ability to dodge in a split second when the need arose.

An older boy who was a swift runner and skillful at dodging was chosen to play the part of the buffalo, deer, mountain lion, or some other animal found in the territory of the tribes playing the game. This player was allowed 10 paces start, and then four to twenty other players gave chase in order to try to strike him on any part of his body with either hand. This game was unlike the usual tag game, since the player who took the part of the animal struck back and any pursuer who was hit by him was out of the game. The pursued player was not content to count coup only on the players who threatened him at close quarters, but he chased those who led the chase and put them out of the running whenever he could. When the game covered a wide area, the player pursued also tried to far outdistance the pursuers at times, in order to test their endurance. Often bands of pursuers who had lost their quarry in the hills far from their village were shamefaced when they returned home to find the boy they had unsuccessfully chased sitting calmly outside a tipi, looking as though he had been there for hours.

A really skillful player would challenge the other players to a contest held within a large circle marked on the ground. This circle would range in size from 50 to 100 feet in diameter. From one to seven opponents tried to count coup on him while he rendered as many of his pursuers *hors de combat* as he could in the shortest time possible. The onlooker shouted "Ho! Ho!" when the pursued player, on being chased by a hunter at top speed, took a short step to one side and struck the outwitted hunter as he passed.

RAIDERS!*

Plains—Woodland—Northwest Coast

BOYS	8 TO 18 PLAYERS	OUTDOORS
JUNIOR—SENIOR	TEAM	

This challenge-game can be carried out with considerable pageantry should a modern chief decide to add a picturesque note. The two bands involved in this contest can march or jog-trot, one group at a time—to avoid a clash even before the actual challenge commences—around the circle, giving blood-curdling war whoops as they advance to their village. When the village is reached, they can stage a war dance, a chief can give a dramatic, gestureful, wordless speech, shaking one or both fists at the braves of the rival village, across the circle from his own. Old clothes, very old clothes, or breech clouts are recommended for the melee.

This challenge should be alertly refereed by two chiefs, preferably neutral, one on either side of the circle, in order to assure that no really strong-arm play is indulged in by either band. The rules can be simple and few. The drawing shows clearly the layout of the terrain and the approximate position of the warriors prior to the "Attack!" shout from the chief in charge. Any contestant who braves the foe by enter-

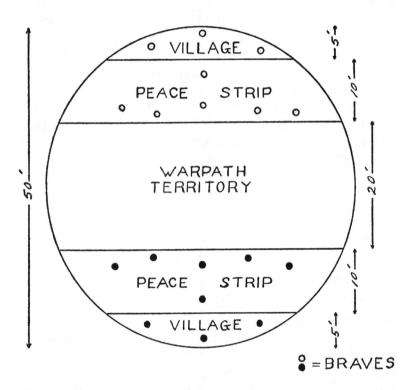

ing the Warpath area is open to capture by the members of the opposing band. He may try to escape or a risky attempt can be made by his band to rescue him in the Peace Strip, but the instant he is pulled or carried into the rival village terrain, he must not attempt to escape nor can he be rescued. Braves of the raiding rescue party can be captured in the enemy's Peace Strip but warriors of the opposing band cannot be captured there, as it is their strip. Should a captured Indian decide to "give up" in order to escape rough handling, which a modern Indian may choose to do, he shouts loudly "I surrender!" and is accompanied by one guard to the enemy village, and cannot be rescued en route. The band with the most prisoners at the end of a certain period, set by the chief in charge, wins.

Even tempers are a big asset in this necessarily rough-and-tumble contest and contestants should bear this in mind or be kept out of these contests by the chief.

5.

Tossing and Catching Games

BOWL CATCH*

Plains—Woodland—Southwest—Northwest Coast

| BOYS OR GIRLS | 4 TO 8 PLAYERS | OUTDOORS |
| ELEMENTARY—JUNIOR | INDIVIDUAL | OR INDOORS |

The Indians of the Americas had many games of chance in which they tossed peach or plum or persimmon pits, beaver or muskrat teeth, or bone and pottery disks—according to the tribe's habitat—from bowls or baskets. These objects bore numbers or designs which established their value. They were jerked upward, usually six at a throw, so that they shot high into the air above the bowl, and the player who had tossed them tried to catch as many as possible when they fell down. The total of the numbers on the objects caught in the bowl, face up, decided the score. In a number of the 130 odd tribes which played this game, the game was usually played by women—and only by women in some tribes. The Indians of the Southwest used special woven baskets, instead of wooden bowls, in which to toss and catch the disks. The players of some tribes jerked the disks, peach pits, or whatever they used, from the bowls by striking the bottom of the bowl on the ground, but most players tossed the objects into the air by throwing them up from the bowl held in both hands.

Here is an adaptation of these games of hazard which should appeal to modern Indians, because skill is mixed with chance, as they will find after they have played the game a few times. The only equipment required to play Bowl Catch is a wooden salad bowl or any other sort of lightweight bowl which has a measurement of 8½ to 12 inches across the top and a depth of about 4 or 5 inches. Instead of using plum stones, modern

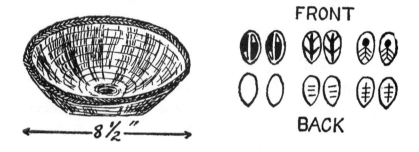

FRONT

BACK

8½"

Indians can make a set of tossing disks by cutting six circles about 1½ inches in diameter from a sheet of heavy cardboard, with numbers marked on each side to indicate the score made on each toss. The numbers may be from 1 to 6 on one side of the disks, with the numbers 2, 4, and 6 on the reverse side of three circles and zero on the other three. A modern chief may use oval disks instead of round ones, if he likes.

The players sit on the ground in a circle with a blanket spread in the center. The chief gives the bowl containing the disks to any player, who is allowed one to three throws, as decided before the game begins. The player can make the throws by bringing the bowl up quickly from lap level and jerking it down again so that the disks fly up into the air. The player must then try to catch as many of them as possible in the bowl as they fall, without changing the sitting position from which they were tossed. The score made on each throw is counted by the chief, who totals all of the numbers shown on the sides of the disks that lie uppermost in the bowl. The bowl is passed clockwise around the circle of seated players as each player completes the throw.

For younger players, the chief may allow them to toss the disks up so that they fall onto the blanket instead of being caught in the bowl, but, of course, this method of play must be used by all players in the circle. Only the sides of disks which fall uppermost on the blanket score in this simple version also.

BOWL TOSS*

Plains—Woodland—Southwest—Northwest Coast

BOYS OR GIRLS   4 TO 8 PLAYERS   OUTDOORS
ELEMENTARY—JUNIOR   INDIVIDUAL—TEAM   OR INDOORS

Here is a further version of the preceding game played in an entirely different way. It is more amusing than Bowl Catch and requires more skill. The same equipment is needed, but two bowls, instead of one, are required. They must be of the same size. The game is played by pairs, and the two players sit directly opposite each other, 4 feet apart. One player has the numbered disks in his bowl and immediately after he calls "Ready!" he tosses the disks, with a sharp jerk of the bowl upward and forward, across to the player sitting opposite him. That player, without changing his sitting position, tries to catch as many of the disks as possible in his bowl, either by pointing the mouth of it toward the disks flying toward him or by trying to place his bowl directly under them, catching them as they fall. Disks missed or disks that fall out of the bowl after they have gone in do not score. Each player can have two or three turns at tossing the disks and the same number of chances to catch the thrown disks. The score is based on the total number shown on the uppermost sides of the disks caught in the bowl. Players should try to toss the disks as well and fairly as possible, knowing that if they toss them to the player opposite them badly they are likely to receive the same treatment when their turn comes to do the catching. The fairest way to conduct this game is for each pair of players to be considered as a partner-team and their joint, total score entered in a contest against the other partner-teams playing.

Some players, with practice, learn to jerk the numbered disks up and forward in such a way that they either fan out or remain grouped at will. As players become more adept at tossing and catching they can be placed farther apart but, naturally, not far enough away from each other to make it difficult to send the disks the required distance.

FIVE STONES TOSS

Southwest

GIRLS	2 TO 10 PLAYERS	OUTDOORS
ELEMENTARY—SENIOR	INDIVIDUAL—TEAM	OR INDOORS

The women of various tribes of the Southwest liked to play and contest this game, which resembles Jackstones somewhat. As the best players contested, their hands moved so fast that it was almost impossible to follow their movements. Let's see how the Pima women played. They used five rounded pebbles, each about 1¼ to 1½ inches in diameter, which were placed conveniently on the ground while the player knelt beside them. She called one of the five stones "My stone," and tossed it straight up into the air, as high as she could, or thought necessary, and then snatched up one stone before the one thrown into the air had fallen. All of the remaining three pebbles are picked up, one at a time, in this way. Should a player miss, her opponent took her turn. Having done the first figure, the next one is to pick up the stones two at a time while the thrown pebble is still in the air. In the next figure, three stones and then the remaining one must be picked up while the thrown pebble is still in air. The last figure, among the ones most suitable for modern Indian maidens, calls for picking up all four stones at once before the tossed pebble hits the ground. Nearly all of the other figures were quite intricate and called for passing the pebbles under finger arches, among other things.

FOX AND GEESE
Northwest Coast

GIRLS	2 TO 10 PLAYERS	OUTDOORS
ELEMENTARY—JUNIOR	INDIVIDUAL	OR INDOORS

This game, which the writer saw being played by two older girls in the Bella Coola territory, in Canada, was played with little figures representing fox, geese, and ducks, carved from bone. In all probability the little figures were of Eskimo origin. It is hard for modern players to get similar figures suitable for the Indian substitute for the game of Jacks, though they can be carved from little blocks of softwood when one has some knowledge of wood carving. This game is mentioned here because it is, like the game which preceded it, an authentic Indian game.

The set used by the Bella Coola girls consisted of a well-carved fox, measuring about 2 inches in length; two geese, each about 1½ inches long; and two ducks, each around 1 inch in length. Each had a base with a flat bottom, instead of the fox and fowl having legs, and they were thrown up into the air from the back or palm of either hand, so that they landed on sand or any smooth piece of ground. Only those which landed in a "standing" position scored. Though the base was heavier than the rest of the figure, having them land in an upright position was a very difficult job! The fox counted 5 points, the geese 3 points each, and the ducks only 1 point each.

WHIRL AND CATCH

Plains—Woodland—Northwest Coast

BOYS OR GIRLS	2 TO 6 PLAYERS	OUTDOORS
ELEMENTARY—JUNIOR	INDIVIDUAL	OR INDOORS

Both boys and girls frequently played this little game, as little preparation or equipment was needed to get a game going. All that was required was six to twelve sticks or reeds about 3 or 4 inches long and from ⅛ to ¼ inch in diameter. In this game, as in others requiring sticks or straws, the lengths of the sticks and their thickness frequently varied slightly. This allows modern Indians some leeway in experimenting to find out which sort of throw sticks they like best. This is how the game is played.

Let us take the easiest way, for younger players, first, for even that is difficult enough. The sticks, from four to twelve, are placed on the back of the hand with the hand held a little above waist level and are then tossed straight up into the air, at least a little higher than the top of the head of the player who tosses them. The falling sticks are then caught on the open palm of the hand which tossed them upward. The fingers and hand must be kept flat or the catch doesn't score. A more difficult way to play is to toss the throw sticks up with the palm or back of the hand and catch them on the back of the open hand when they fall. Many Indian youngsters can do that without difficulty and go on to the final and most difficult way of playing throw sticks. They toss the sticks up as before but whirl around, once, rapidly before catching the falling sticks on the back of the hand. Modern players should start with only a few sticks and work up to a dozen!

COME BACK BALL

Northwest Coast

GIRLS	4 PLAYERS	OUTDOORS
JUNIOR—SENIOR	INDIVIDUAL	OR INDOORS

The older girls of some of the Northwest Coast tribes were fond of this game and played it very expertly. Not only did they bounce the ball with surprising speed and precision, using the palm of either hand, but, when it was prearranged, they used an agile foot or knee when it suited them. They also played the game with greater distances between the sides of the square on which they stood and the bouncing point than those given below. This is how the game may best be played by modern Indians, and with a far better, bouncier ball than the homemade ones or round, inflated sea mammal bladders used by the Indian girls.

Four girls stand each at the center of one of the sides of a 12-foot square marked out on the play area. Directly in the center of the square, a circle of 12 inches in diameter is marked. Each girl faces her rival across the square and the mode of play is to keep a volleyball or basketball bouncing from the palm of one hand to the center spot and on to the girl opposite, and the ball is bounced back in the same way. A bad stroke which makes it impossible for the girl opposite to return it may count as one miss. When any girl misses the ball three times, the ball goes to the other pair of players.

Another form of play is for all four girls to keep the ball bouncing back and foward across the square so that it remains in play for as long a time as possible. Three misses and out is the rule for this method of play also. A girl from the side lines can take the place of a player who drops out. Without forcing the play, good players can keep the ball in constant motion for several minutes at a time.

A double hazard version of this game is to have each two

players use a volleyball and when one ball has been knocked three times out of the square by the ball of the other pair of players, the pair who has forced the ball out three times counts coup and wins.

This game can also be played very well with a tennis ball or any other sort of rubber ball of similar size, provided it bounces well.

HANDICAP BALL TOSS*

Northwest Coast

BOYS OR GIRLS   3 TO 12 PLAYERS   OUTDOORS
ELEMENTARY—JUNIOR   INDIVIDUAL

When a Northwest Coast Indian boy was given the round bladder of a sea mammal by a hunter, the first thing he did after he had inflated it was to find as many ways as possible to use it to amuse himself, especially when conditions sometimes caused him to play alone a good deal. He threw the bladder, he headed it, he kicked it, and experimented to see how many ways he could toss it and keep advancing while doing so. Here is one of many ways in which modern chiefs can have their Indians contest in a Handicap Ball Toss race.

Each boy is given a soccerball, volleyball, or basketball. Players stand 6 feet apart behind a starting line marked on the ground, facing another line at least 90 feet away. On the word "Go!" each player tosses the ball, while facing forward, with both hands, one hand holding it in front of his opened legs while the other hand holds it from behind the legs. He then runs forward, picks the ball up and, for the second toss, again throws it between his legs from behind but only with the right hand this time. The third toss is made, when the ball has been reached and picked up, by tossing it from behind between opened legs with the left hand. All of these tosses are made while facing the finish line, and the player runs as fast as possible between each toss in order to arrive at the finish line as soon as possible.

Should the chief decide to let the contestants lengthen the race by racing back to the starting line, after having reached the second line, they make all throws with their backs to the starting line, using the same sequence of throws as they did on the first lap of the race. Strangely enough, most tossers will find it easier to toss the ball further when throwing from this position. After each throw, the tossers turn and run forward to recover the balls, then turn and make the throw from the backward position.

With sufficient referees, this game is best played by making each player throw from where the ball landed, not from where it rolled. The first player to reach the finish line decided on counts coup and wins. Some judgment is needed in order to make good time in this race, and straight throwing is also a big help.

SHIELD AND BALL*

Plains

BOYS	2 TO 6 PLAYERS	OUTDOORS
JUNIOR—SENIOR	INDIVIDUAL	OR INDOORS

The Omaha and other warriors of the Plains tribes used circular shields, usually made of raw buffalo hide. They were often effective against arrows which were not fired at point-blank range, as arrows fired at close range were able to go entirely through a buffalo. These shields also turned aside hatchet strokes and lance thrusts. With the Indians' well-developed sense of the artistic, they covered these shields with a cover of deerskin that fitted snugly over the shield. These covers bore various paintings, frequently depicting a vision which had appeared to the shield owner while fasting. All of this serves as an introduction to the game, for had there been

113

no shields, there would have been no ideas for games with shields.

When some of the older boys of the tribes could borrow, make, or find a discarded shield that was not too heavy, they needed only to locate a few rawhide-covered balls and the game could begin. Of course, a shield in current use was never used for any play purpose until its cover was removed and not, as a rule, even then. Once the players were equipped, however, a 30 or 40 foot circle was marked on the ground and the shield bearer stood in the center of it, holding the shield by its arm sling inside. The other players stood just outside the circle, at any point or points, and threw the balls at the young warrior who had to protect himself against these fast-flying missiles by the adept use of the shield, coupled with dodging and jumping. Usually each player had a ball to throw, but when players stood on opposite sides of the circle, they threw any ball which came their way. The player who first hit the shield bearer on any part of the body, *not* the shield, took his place. Sometimes three or six hits had to be scored by a player before the shield man was considered *hors de combat*. The player who had scored the most hits took his place in the middle of the circle.

Modern players can contest in this way. A round shield, about 20 or 24 inches in diameter, can be made from light plywood or even very strong, reinforced cardboard. A sling made from a strip of leather or strong cloth about 8 inches long is fastened to the center of the shield, inside. This serves as a handgrip by which the shield is held and maneuvered as protection from the flying balls. Let's suppose that the challenger, with the shield, is being attacked by four other players standing just outside a 40-foot circle marked on the ground. Each attacker can be armed with a soft or sponge rubber ball ranging in size from 2 to 4 inches in diameter; or only one or two balls may be thrown, as decided by the chief. It is easiest for the throwers, from the viewpoint of fielding the balls, to stand at the four points of the compass, one thrower posted in the North, and one at each of the other three cardinal points. When the chief shouts "Attack!" the throwers begin to throw the number of balls in use at the shield bearer in the middle of the circle. A ball may be retrieved from anywhere within the circle, but no ball may be thrown from anywhere inside the circle. The chief, to speed up the contest, may appoint one or two boys who are not playing at the moment to pick up and throw the balls that go astray back to the throwers. The chief keeps a keen eye on the hits made, and by whom, and decides on the scoring system to be used before the next shield bearer, who has counted coup by the number of hits scored, gets his turn in the ring.

Interesting variations of this challenge-game can be carried out by increasing or decreasing the distance from which the balls are thrown and also by having the attackers use much larger balls, such as volleyballs, as missiles. In such cases, one ball will be sufficient ammunition, but the chief must see that the throwers get turn about rather than one player throwing several times in succession. The larger balls, thrown from over the head with one or both hands, provide good sport.

SHIELD ON SHIELD*

Plains

BOYS	2 TO 6 PLAYERS	OUTDOORS
JUNIOR—SENIOR	INDIVIDUAL	OR INDOORS

When young Indians were fortunate enough to come by two shields, they were equipped to play a shield tossing game which required some skill and strength when the game was played for a long period without a break. When only one shield was to be found, they made a second shield of the same size as the first from wood or bark, or a still easier substitute was resorted to by simply marking the outline of a shield on the ground. Sometimes this circle was the exact size of the regular shield they were going to use, and at others it was from 3 to 6 inches in diameter larger. From a throwing mark ranging from 12 to 20 feet distant, the throwers tossed the shield, held flat, with one hand, in the way which came easiest to them. The object of the game was to land the thrown shield directly on top of the other shield, or circle, so that it remained there. The distance used for scoring was measured from where the shield first fell, flat, on the ground. A shield which landed on its edge before falling over on its side did not score. The thrower who counted coup was the one who first landed the shield three times, or more, as decided, directly on the mark. Of course these throws were not necessarily made in succession.

Modern chiefs will be able to play this game in the best way to suit the throwers' size and strength.

REBOUND

Northwest Coast

BOYS   3 TO 6 PLAYERS   OUTDOORS
JUNIOR—SENIOR   INDIVIDUAL—TEAM

Indian men and boys of many tribes played a number of games which may be classed as Rebound Games. In these games they threw light, straight sticks, such as sumac or red willow, against tree stumps, logs, or rocks in order to have the sticks either bound back or, more frequently, ricochet and fall as far from the object used to cause the rebound as possible. Often the sticks were so light and cleverly cut that the breeze considerably aided their long flights. The only possible danger in such games is that a thrower or incautious bystander can be struck by a rebound or ricochet. In every possible form of game where there is the slightest risk of any sort involved, no matter how remotely, the modern leader, adopting *Better safe than sorry!* for his motto, will either strike such a game from his games repertoire or conduct it in such a way that risk is entirely eliminated. The chance of anyone being struck by a rebound in this game, if played as suggested, is about one in a thousand. The more cautious leaders may consider even this too great a risk! Here is how Rebound was played by the Kwakiutl.

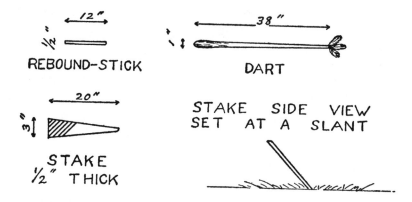

REBOUND-STICK

DART

STAKE ½" THICK

STAKE SIDE VIEW
SET AT A SLANT

They drove a pointed slat, shaped as in the drawing, firmly into the ground. Sometimes they used two stakes, one 21½ and the other 15½ inches long. These slat-stakes were only 1½ inches wide at the top, but that was plenty wide enough, because the Indians who played the game were dead shots with the darts they threw. The stake in the drawing is wider, to provide a less discouraging target for modern Indians. These stakes were cut from a strip of thin, strong, very springy wood. Though a number of suitable thin woods are available today, makeshift slats, which serve quite well, can be cut from the thin, springy slats of various fruit crates. The author watched Indian boys bounce short, straight, hardwood stakes about 10 inches long and at least ½ inch thick, sideways, against the stake, using both hands for the throw. They did it so accurately, throwing from a distance of about 10 feet, that they nearly always caught the stick, with one or both hands, on the rebound.

The real throwing darts of the Kwakiutl were made of hardwood. They were heavy and perfectly balanced. One dart was 35 inches long and the other 38 inches long, with an ingenious rattle skillfully built into the handle end. This was a simple feat for people who ranked very high among the world's best wood carvers. Instead of the rattler, the drawing suggests three fluffy feathers glued into the thin end of the dart to aid its straight flight. The throwing range of the Northwest Coast Indians was from 20 to 40 feet. It is suggested that modern Indians start at minimum range until throwing skill is developed. The Indians did not score unless they caught the dart on its rebound; however, this rule can easily be eliminated by the modern Indians, along with the risk of being struck by a dart on the rebound. In this case, the game is judged on the basis of accuracy, and the thrower who first scores three or six direct hits on the stake, followed by good rebounds, wins.

The drawings are based on the adaptation of the game and will be found suitable for making the equipment required for modern play. Chiefs can experiment with the angles at which the stake can be driven into the ground. Different slants produce widely different results and some of them will be found to throw the darts almost straight up into the air. This is quite an adult game and older players will find that the amount of entertainment it provides is worth the small amount of time and trouble necessary to make the equipment.

PONY RIDE*

Southwest

BOYS	4 TO 8 PLAYERS	OUTDOORS
JUNIOR—SENIOR	TEAM	OR INDOORS

This is a stone-throwing game which the Pima onlookers enjoyed as much as the players. How these Indian men played the game is told first; then a version for modern Indians, which is perfectly safe and easily staged, follows. The Pima players dug two holes directly opposite each other and 50 feet apart. The holes were 2 feet deep and about 15 inches across at the top. Two players, each provided with a large, roundish stone about 6 inches in diameter, stood at each hole. Each two men were a team. A member of the team chosen to throw first, tossed a stone in an effort to land it squarely in the hole opposite. The stone had to drop in, not roll in. The two members of the team who were not throwing *did not* stand a safe distance away from the hole under fire. One of them being put out of the running by a heavy stone falling on his foot was always cause for much laughter, in which the victim joined. If either member of the tossing team put a stone into the hole, he and his partner were carried on their rivals' backs across to the hole in which the stone landed, and the teams changed ends. When both players on one team each put a stone in the hole, in succession, then both of these players were carried by their opponents to the hole in which the stones landed and back again to the hole from which the stones were tossed, not changing ends in this case. The men who carried their rivals acted like trotting horses, performing antics which convulsed the onlookers, while the victors tried to look dignified and appeared completely indifferent to the capers of their mettlesome steeds, no matter how badly they were shaken up on the trip.

The following version of the game can be played by modern Indians. It is easier to play because no holes need be dug, and

119

much safer than the carefree Indian style of play. Two pails take the place of the two holes, and two or four volleyballs or basketballs take the place of the stones. Smaller balls, soft or semihard, from 2 to 6 inches in diameter, can take the place of the larger balls if necessary. The scoring can be the same as in the Indian version, and landing the balls in the pails is more difficult than throwing them into the holes in the ground. Since the writer is violently opposed to any game in which youngsters are carried on each other's backs, horseback fashion, because of the many serious accidents resulting from that form of "play" which he hears about as he stages games demonstrations in various cities, it is suggested that the "horseback" mode of forfeit be dropped from this game. Instead, those who score may still be honored with a ride—and bounced around a little too—by the losers carrying them in any of the three first-aid carrying seats, which are doubtless known to all games leaders. In case a novice does not, this is how these chairs are made.

First, the two-handed seat. Let's call the two carrying players A and B for easy identification. A grasps B's left wrist with his right hand, while B grasps A's wrist with his left hand, or the left and right hands may be finger-hooked instead, and the free hands are placed on each other's shoulders. The arms provide a comfortable back rest for the player being carried.

The three-handed seat is formed by A grasping his own left wrist with his right hand and B's right wrist with his left hand. B then grasps A's right wrist with his right hand and places his left hand on A's shoulder, so that the arm forms a back rest.

The four-handed seat is formed as in the three-hand carry, except that B grasps his own left wrist with his right hand and A's right wrist with his left hand. This makes a comfortable but backless seat. The person being carried places his arms around the carriers' necks and shoulders for additional support.

HOOP TOSS

Plains

BOYS	2 TO 8 PLAYERS	OUTDOORS
ELEMENTARY—JUNIOR	INDIVIDUAL	

When a Lakotah boy could get hold of a hoop that a dancer had discarded, he was glad to get it and used it in a number of different ways. Copying some of the dancers, he would see how often he could twirl the hoop around his ankle without its falling off. He would then twirl it around his wrist. When he became tired of these dance movements, he devised a game

121

which provides fun and difficulty enough to amuse and test a modern Indian. Let's see how we can play this hoop game.

The only equipment required is one or, better still, several light, wooden hoops each somewhere from 15 to 20 inches in diameter. If wooden barrel hoops, or store hoops, are not available, hoops can easily be made from suitable lengths of straight willow or other supple branches, long enough to make the hoop needed and about ½ inch, or a little more, thick. These lengths can be joined nicely at the two ends by thinning each end so that they both lie flat and can be whipped firmly together. The hoops will still serve even if the join is not too professional a job. A pole 5 feet long and about 1 or 1½ inches in diameter is pointed at one end and driven about 12 inches into the ground. Then, from a throwing line 15 feet distant, for a start, the throwers try to toss the hoop. with either hand, over the pole, so that it encircles it and falls to the ground with the pole still inside the hoop.

With lightweight, well-made hoops, this game is amusing and not too easy, since most of the ring tossing done these days is in games such as quoits, where the throw is downward, and much easier than one made over a stake with the top 4 feet above ground level. In successfully encircling the pole at this height, the hoop must be tossed with sufficient skill to send the side of the hoop nearest the pole just over it, with the side furthest from the pole at a lower level so that it hits the pole and causes the hoop to drop over it. This throw, hard as it may appear to be, is, with some practice, easier to accomplish than a straight upward throw so well-judged that the hoop drops exactly over the pole with no part of the hoop striking the pole while encircling it. The winner is the thrower who first encircles the pole three or six times, as decided in advance.

PINE CONE HOOP TOSS

Northwest Coast—Plains—Woodland—Southwest

ELEMENTARY—JUNIOR   3 TO 12 PLAYERS   OUTDOORS

BOYS OR GIRLS   INDIVIDUAL   OR INDOORS

There was probably no Indian youngster of the Americas who did not play some sort of game with pine cones of various sorts as the chief or only equipment required. The Indian players of the West Coast had the fine 15-inch long sugar pine cones to play with, those in the Northeast and Great Lakes area had white pine cones, and when Indian fathers felled lodgepole pines, yes, for lodge poles, some Plains Indian children had the almost indestructible cones as playthings. These children played catch with the cones, held throwing contests to find the champion throwers for height, distance, and accuracy, and played various forms of Duck on a Rock with them, among many other things.

Here is a game for modern Indians that will test their accuracy as well as the ability to make long tosses. A hoop of any sort, ranging in size from 12 to 18 inches, or even larger if the modern Indians who play this game live in the sugar pine region, is the first requirement. This hoop can easily be made from long grasses or supple reeds, or by bending a flexible willow branch into a circle of the required size and then tying the two ends together. The hoop is placed on the ground 12 feet away, for a start, from a throwing line, which can be a mark on the ground or a straight branch. Each player stands just behind this line, is given three pine cones and allowed to make three underhand tosses in attempts to drop each cone inside the hoop. One point can be allowed for cones falling inside the ring and then bouncing out, and 3 points for each cone which remains inside the circle. The hoop is gradually moved farther and farther away from the throwing line as the throwers develop accuracy and know-how. Of course Indian

123

children tried tossing the cones with each hand and then from between legs placed wide apart, with back toward the target.

As a grand finale, modern chiefs may hang the hoop from the limb of a tree, so that it is about 10 feet above ground level, and have the throwers try their skill for accuracy by throwing the pine cones through the hoops from various distances.

WOODPECKER*

Woodland

BOYS OR GIRLS   2 TO 6 PLAYERS   OUTDOORS
ELEMENTARY—JUNIOR   INDIVIDUAL   OR INDOORS

The writer watched some Indian children in the Woodland area trying to throw fir cones into a small hole in the trunk of a tree. The hole was about 2 inches in diameter and 15 feet above ground level. The boys and girls took turns at throwing, except when a player managed to put a cone into the hole. When this happened, and it happened fairly often, the player continued to throw until he missed. The players threw fast, overhand, standing about 3 paces away from the bottom of the trunk of the tree, and did not use the easier method of a slow, underhand toss. The players said that they were playing Woodpecker. Each cone going into the hole represented a woodpecker flying into its nest. The first player to get nine cones into the hole counted coup.

An adaptation of this game which makes it easy to play indoors or outdoors can be played as follows. A chief can make a woodpecker's nest by cutting a hole about 2½ or 3 inches in diameter in the lid of a big, strong cardboard box. A box anywhere from 12 to 24 inches in diameter will do. After the hole is made in the box lid, the lid can be glued on to the box and the box hung on a wall or pole so that it is suspended from 15 to 20 feet above ground level. Instead of fir cones, the players can throw small rubber or paper balls about 1½ inches in diameter. The players stand just behind a line marked on the floor or ground about 10 feet away from where the foot of the tree trunk would be. The first player to put six balls into the hole counts coup. Should a ball bounce out of the "nest," which is unlikely, it does not score.

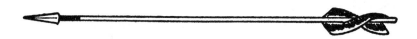

BLANKET, BASKET, BALL*
Southwest

BOYS OR GIRLS	8 TO 24 PLAYERS	OUTDOORS
JUNIOR—SENIOR	INDIVIDUAL	OR INDOORS

The Navaho of Arizona played a game called *Ashbii* in which they tossed short sticks underhand, while seated, against a blanket stretched tightly above their heads by being fastened to the walls of the hogan, the name of the dwelling in which this tribe lived. They sat in a square formation around the suspended blanket and a basket was placed directly in the middle of the square, with the blanket directly above on which to bounce the sticks. The sticks, thrown one at a time against the blanket, scored the various points which their markings represented, provided they fell into and remained in the basket. Sticks that missed the basket or bounded out after falling into it did not score.

This is how modern Indians can enjoy this amusing game, which requires skill and judgment in tossing the sticks, as well as luck. The equipment required is a blanket, a big tablecloth, or a piece of strong cloth about 6 feet square, or a round piece of cloth 6 feet in diameter will serve just as well. A round basket or a wooden bowl, measuring about 18 inches in diameter across the top and an inside height of around 6 inches, completes the simple gear, with the exception of three smooth sticks 4 inches long, 1 inch wide, and about ⅜ inch thick, or three small rubber balls about 1 or 1½ inches in diameter can be used instead. The sticks or balls can be numbered 1, 4, and 6 by either marking the numbers directly on them with an indelible pencil or by marking the numbers on small pieces of adhesive tape and sticking them onto the sticks or balls.

To play the game, two to six players sit on each side of the square, with the blanket directly above them. The easiest way to keep the blanket above the modern Indian players, who may not have a hogan handy, is to have four other players, who should be given the opportunity to play the next game, hold the blanket tightly stretched and at shoulder height above the seated players. Indian players had the blanket considerably higher than this, but the end results are very much the same. A player in the North end of the square is given the three sticks or balls and proceeds to toss them underhand one at a time against the blanket, hitting it at any point from which he believes it will be most likely to bounce back into the basket underneath. After that player has had three throws and his score has been marked by a tally keeper, the sticks are passed on to the next player. They go clockwise around the square until each player has had a chance to score. Luck enters into the game because of the differently numbered sticks. If sticks without numbers are used and each stick bounced into the basket counts 1 point, the element of luck affects the scoring considerably less.

When balls are used instead of sticks, it is best to use either a small wastepaper basket or pail to catch the bouncing balls, as they are fairly certain to bounce out of a basket or bowl with low sides. If only a basket is available, some grass or excelsior placed in the bottom of it will assure that the balls bounce less. Of course, should the modern player desire further handicap, the basket or bowl can be used without either grass or excelsior in the bottom of it. Scores may be considerably lower but there will be more fun. Quite a lot of skill is required to bounce the ball from blanket to basket, as players will soon discover.

A total of anywhere from 30 to 50 points can be set as the winning score.

CORNCOB RING TOSS

Southwest—Plains—Woodland

BOYS OR GIRLS	3 TO 18 PLAYERS	OUTDOORS
ELEMENTARY—JUNIOR	INDIVIDUAL—TEAM	

Many Indian youngsters of widely spread Indian nations and tribes played games of various sorts with corncobs. An amusing corncob tossing game of the Pueblo children appears elsewhere in this chapter. Were it not for the author's intense dislike of "playthings" which should actually be listed in the "dangerous weapon" category, the game of corncob darts might be recorded here. Instead, a game follows which the author saw played in the Southwest by a group of Indian children who counted only on Mother Nature to furnish their playthings. This game does *not* require a dangerous, steel-pointed dart but does require as much skill as the omitted dart game.

In order to eliminate wastefulness—the eyes of so many hungry children would light up if they were given an ear of sweet corn—let us use only what is left after the kernels have been eaten. The corncob should be washed well. One end of the cob is heavier than the other, so it is that end that travels first when the dart is in flight. About ½ inch is cut from the thin end of the cob, then three small holes are bored, in a triangle pattern, straight down into that end of the cob. One well-feathered chicken feather is pushed, quill-end down, into each hole and the harmless, blunt-ended dart is ready for use.

Fluffy feathers such as the ones usually found in feather dusters make good flight feathers, if a discarded feather mop is available. The Hopi children, let it be told, neither cut the end off the corncob nor bored holes in it. They simply tied three or four feathers onto the thin end of the improvised dart with fiber-grass.

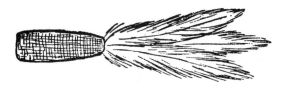

The target at which these darts are tossed is either a clearly marked ring drawn on the ground or a wooden hoop ring made from a thin, flexible branch of desired length, bent into a circle and the two ends tied securely together with a piece of strong twine. The great advantage of the wooden hoop is that it can be either laid flat on the ground or, braced by a thin stake on either side, stood on end, at any angle, in order to form varied targets. This hoop target can also be suspended at any required height from the branch of a tree and the darts thrown through it to score. The wooden ring has still another advantage, for it can be made in any size required in a few moments so that smaller targets can be used by good shots and larger targets for novices.

The dart tossers stand just behind a throwing line from 12 to 30 feet away from the circle used as a ground target and try to land three darts inside the circle in three consecutive throws. The chief can decide on the score, and whether darts which actually land and remain within the circle, instead of bouncing out, should score extra points or not. The Indian youngsters threw at the ground target by letting the dart lie flat in the hand with the feathers toward the body, of course, and the heavy end close to the finger tips. Drawing the hand backward, and crooking the fingers slightly to hold the dart in place, the hand and arm was thrust forcibly forward, sending the dart in a straight line for a surprising distance. When they threw the dart at a distant hoop target suspended from a tree branch, they held it between thumb and two fingers, from the over-the-shoulder position. These simple darts fly quite well, and distance and accuracy can be assured with some practice.

TOES CORNCOB TOSS

Southwest

BOYS   4 TO 8 PLAYERS   OUTDOORS
ELEMENTARY—JUNIOR   INDIVIDUAL

This is an amusing game which pleased Pueblo Indian boys, after the corn crop had been harvested. The following is a simple account of how the game may be played, without going into the elaborate ceremonials which often took place before the game got under way.

There was an ear of corn for each contestant and each ear was either differently colored or marked for identification in some other way. About 1½ inches of stalk was left on each ear of corn, for a toe grip. The throwers lay on their backs, side by side, with about one pace between them. Their feet were bare, of course, and each boy placed the stalk end of his corncob between the big toe and the one next to it, using either foot, with the ear of corn pointing away from the sole of the foot and held firmly between the toes. The legs were touching the ground.

When a chief shouted "Throw!" each boy brought the leg and foot which held the corncob up, as forcibly as he could, releasing the corncob so that it flew over his head and traveled as far as possible. A chief ceremoniously paced off the distance to which the farthest-thrown cobs had traveled in order to decide the winner. Modern Indians will find that the distance to which a corncob can be thrown in the manner described increases greatly with a little practice. The leg that does not help to propel the cob is best held close to the ground for balance.

Pueblo boys sometimes staged contests of their own in which they threw the corncobs in the opposite direction, by bringing the throwing leg up as far toward the head as possible and then tossing the cob by jerking the leg sharply downward.

Tossing and Catching Games

Modern Indians can try both methods and the chief may decide that each thrower can throw three times in succession, the total distance thrown being counted as each thrower's score. These days, it is wise for a chief to dip the stalk end of the corncob in an antiseptic solution, then dry it off, if it is going to be thrown by more than one boy. Pueblo boys never suffered from athlete's foot!

6.

Throwing and Rolling Games

ALL IN AIR*

Plains

BOYS OR GIRLS	2 TO 6 PLAYERS	OUTDOORS
ELEMENTARY—SENIOR	INDIVIDUAL	OR INDOORS

This game is an adaptation of a game played by the Mandan and many other Indian tribes, sometimes called the Game of the Arrow, in which a brave fired as many arrows as possible high and straight up into the air so that the greatest number of arrows were in the air, at any height, at the same time. Since the arrows used were often heavy war arrows, most of them were shot out of sight, and all of them had to come down sooner or later, this is *not* a game to be recommended to archery clubs or modern young Robin Hoods.

This adaptation is safer and it too requires quite a lot of skill. It is played with small, hard rubber balls, 1 or 1½ inches in diameter, which cost very little. At least eight of these balls will be required for each group of players. Though the Mandan bowman clutched eight or ten arrows in his left hand, the modern player need only hold four to six balls in the hand which is not used for throwing. Since this may prove too many balls for too small a hand, in the case of little players, the balls may be held in a rather deep paper plate instead. The other players form a big circle around the first thrower and when he is ready, the chief calls "Throw!"

The player then throws as many balls as fast as he can and as straight up and as high as he can, one ball after another into the air. As soon as one of the thrown balls strikes the ground, the chief who starts the game and acts as referee, announces the number of balls that were in the air at the same time. Another player in the circle then takes his turn at throwing, and so on until all of the players in the circle have had a chance to compete. The player who has had the largest number of balls in the air at the same time counts coup and wins.

FLYING FEATHER

Plains—Woodland—Northwest Coast—Southwest

| BOYS OR GIRLS | 2 TO 12 PLAYERS | OUTDOORS |
| ELEMENTARY—JUNIOR | INDIVIDUAL | OR INDOORS |

Probably all of the Indian boys and girls of the Americas played some games in which they used big feathers, such as goose, swan, or wild turkey feathers, as darts. These were thrown at varied targets in various ways and from different distances. These heavily quilled feathers flew for a long distance, especially when aided by a following breeze, and traveled with astonishing accuracy when thrown by a skilled hand, rendered adept through practice. Practically no Indian boy could resist throwing a long, dartlike feather which lay temptingly in his path, and there were plenty of feathers in those days. He threw such feathers for distance, height, and accuracy, probably ending by launching one neatly into a hole high up in a big tree, perhaps to the annoyance of the raccoon, squirrel, or woodpecker who lived there.

Modern chiefs can do quite as well as these Indian feather fliers, though suitable feathers are far scarcer today. This is how it can be done. Any long, full-feathered feather makes a good start in the direction of a Flying Feather Contest. Once the feather is in hand, the chief winds one or two narrow strips of thin, flexible lead, such as is used for sinkers on fishing lines, around the extreme end of the quill. To make a finished, artistic job, of which an Indian could be proud, the lead strip is entirely covered by wrapping a length of colored twine or wool around it. The feather is now ready to fly fast, far, and accurately, when thrown well. It can also be used as the chief requirement for the Magic Feather Dance* at any outdoor or

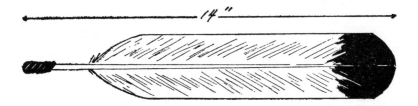

indoor Indian Council Fire. This finished feather should be classed by wise chiefs as a dangerous weapon, though it does not compare in deadliness with the store-bought, steel-pointed darts, for the feather dart, though blunt-pointed, when thrown forcibly at close quarters can cause some regrettable injury which need never happen when all such feather darts are used with precaution and under supervision.

Flying Feather Contests may be staged in a number of ways. Throwing for distance is carried out by throwing the feather from a spot marked on the ground as far as possible in a straight line. Throwing for height can be done close, but not too close, to some tall tree that will help to mark the height to which each feather dart flies. A good way to test accuracy of throw is to have the contestants throw the feather from a mark

* See *Camp Fire and Council Ring Programs,* Allan A. Macfarlan (New York: Association Press, 1951) pp. 114–115.

on the ground through a small wooden or withe hoop, about 9 inches in diameter, suspended from a branch or overhead line of string, so that the bottom of the hoop is about 6 feet above ground level. A wide field opens here, as the hoop targets, of various sizes, can be thrown at from distances varying from 15 feet to as much as 30 feet, or placed flat on the ground at a distance of 20 feet from the throwing point to test skill at flight from space to target. Fancy flying can be indulged in by having the more efficient contestants endeavor to throw the feather so that it travels in a circle, boomerang fashion, from the throwing point. Indian boys, especially the Nootka of the Canadian Northwest Coast, can make such feathers travel in a complete circle, without apparent difficulty.

Modern chiefs should experiment with the weight of the lead strip or strips attached to the point of various feathers, as sometimes a very light strip of lead will make for fancier flying than a heavier strip, which is best suited to carry a feather dart swiftly and directly to a fixed target at fairly long range.

CLOWN BALL*

Southwest

BOYS	12 TO 30 PLAYERS	OUTDOORS
ELEMENTARY—JUNIOR	TEAM	OR INDOORS

It is only fair to begin by saying that the Zuni clowns were first-rate merrymakers and much brighter than their role and dress seemed to indicate. This is one of the games in which they played a prominent part for the amusement of the People of the Pueblos. While the clowns' antics as they played appeared to be clumsy and laughable, an alert onlooker could see how cleverly they bluffed and dodged and threw their opponents off balance, to avoid being hit by the ball.

The game was played in this way. A long center line was

drawn on the ground from North to South and the outline filled in with colored corn meal. Another line was drawn on each side of this central line and at a distance of 15 feet from it. The players lined up, 3 feet apart, one half standing just outside the eastern side of the line and the other half standing just outside the line on the West. One side was given a semi-hard ball, covered with cotton cloth, which measured 6 inches in diameter. A player on the side with the ball ran to the center line and tried to hit a player on the opposing team with the ball. If that player was hit, he went over to the thrower's team and the successful thrower continued to throw until he missed. The rival team then took over, and the game continued until all of one team had been put out of business and forced to join the opposing team.

This often took several hours, of course, which is one reason why the writer suggests that a chief who referees this game for modern Indians call a halt after ten or fifteen minutes of play and award the game to the side with the most players, or let it carry on for another ten minutes or so. The chief may also decide to lengthen the distance between the lines and have the players throw a volleyball, with one or two hands, instead of a smaller ball, such as a tennis ball.

A similar game, played with a wool ball, is contested by various tribes. Sometimes a player from the side which does not hold the ball is called to the center line. He then turns his back to the thrower on the other team, who remains in line with his team and throws the ball from that position. If the player thrown at is hit, he joins the thrower's team, but if he is missed, the ball goes to his team and he is given the next chance to throw the ball at a member of the opposing team.

THREE-THROW BALL*

Plains—Southwest

BOYS   2 TO 6 PLAYERS   OUTDOORS
JUNIOR—SENIOR   INDIVIDUAL   OR INDOORS

This game is an adaptation of a game played by many of
the Plains People. Though they played with only the one-
throw method, this adaptation triples the fun by introducing
a three-throw way of play. The ball used should be a soft
rubber ball of about the size of a tennis ball, which serves very
well. The player lies on his back so that the top of his head
touches a line drawn on the ground. Several players can contest
at the same time, with about 3 feet between the players. The
hands of the player are stretched out by his sides, with the
hands close to the knees. The chief then hands him a ball and
he makes three throws, for distance, throwing the ball behind
him while lying flat on his back during the throw. Each throw
is measured for distance. One throw is made with the left
hand, one with the right hand, and one using both hands. For
all of these throws, the player stretches his arms downward
so that the hands reach close to the knees. A strict rule is that
each throw must be made with both shoulders resting flat on
the ground. This is the "catch" in the game, as the throwing
position makes a long throw by any method quite difficult. As
the handicap is the same for each thrower, the game plays no
favorites.

Throwers will discover that, with a little practice, there is

138

an art in throwing the ball from this flat-on-the-ground position and that releasing the ball at exactly the right moment will add considerable distance to the throws. The throws are all for length, and the place where the ball first strikes the ground decides the total distance thrown.

Some of the tribes used to attach short throwing-thongs about 10 inches long to the leather cover of these throwing balls, but modern Indians will find that they can get along very well without these additions. The modern chief will find that this game can be made even more amusing by occasionally substituting a volleyball or basketball for the tennis-type ball. Another variation is to let the players throw the ball from above their heads, sending it forward instead of backward, while lying in the flat-on-the-ground position.

HIT THE STONE*

Northwest Coast

BOYS   2 TO 6 PLAYERS   OUTDOORS
ELEMENTARY—SENIOR   INDIVIDUAL

The Haida warriors and boys, whose warlike way of life necessitated their being handy with every possible weapon in an emergency, were adept at throwing stones. They stood a heavy stone, measuring about 12 inches high and from 2 to 3 inches in width, on end on the ground and threw heavy, round, ball-like stones at it from distances ranging from 20 to 40 feet. Usually groups of two to six players took part in these contests, and the first player to knock the stone over ten times, not necessarily in succession, counted coup. As a rule they took turn about at throwing, but sometimes the chief allowed a player to continue throwing as long as he knocked the stone down with each throw.

Modern Indians will find equally good exercise and training in marksmanship by throwing a rubber ball, about the size of a tennis ball, at an individual-size cereal package filled with earth or sand. This target should be set up on a level piece of ground which allows a throwing range of from 10 to 40 feet, the distance being based on the age and skill of the throwers. A wooden block, the same size as the stone used by the Haida, can replace the cereal package filled with earth. The players take turns at throwing the ball. The scoring used by the Haida may be adopted and a player who knocks the target over may be allowed to continue until he misses. Since the important part of this game is to develop a throw which packs a wallop, balls must be thrown overhand.

CROW ARROW THROW

Plains

BOYS	2 TO 6 PLAYERS	OUTDOORS
ELEMENTARY—JUNIOR	INDIVIDUAL	

Before he could contest this game, the Indian boy had first of all to make a good throwing arrow. This is how he did it. He cut a straight piece of wild cherry 4 feet long and about 1 inch thick. If he could not find cherry, he used a slim, straight gray birch or maple sapling instead. He tapered the shaft from its original thickness at the thick end, at least 1 inch, to ⅜ inch at the thin end. After most of the surplus wood has been shaved off with a knife or drawknife, a piece of coarse emery paper, instead of rough sand, will complete the job for the modern Indian, except for the final smooth over-all finish. The arrow may be oiled or colored when this stage is reached.

The distance to which the arrow can be thrown can be considerably increased by wrapping a thin strip or two of flexible lead around the heavy end of the arrow and whipping it securely in place with a length of colored twine. Strong twine and careful whipping may be further strengthened by giving it a coat of clear varnish, or waxing it. The arrow should now be carefully balanced on the finger to find its point of balance. This spot should be marked. Starting about 1 inch above the mark, strong, colored twine should be wrapped carefully around the arrow, each strand touching the other, to a point 2 inches below the mark. This provides a 3-inch throwing grip. Two big feathers, from a goose or turkey, should be carefully split down the center, as for fletching regular arrows. Either two or three of the best pieces, each 6 inches long, should be glued or bound on with very thin, waxed twine, at equal distances apart, with the top of the feathers about 1 inch from the top of the slim end of the arrow, which is now ready for use.

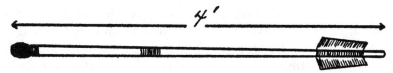

The Crow not only competed for accuracy in throwing this arrow but also held contests for distance throwing. The contestant who counted coup for the long-distance throw was decided by the best out of three throws, in a straight line. Modern Indians who contest should be certain that their arrows are close to the same weight and construction as those of their opponents, to assure fair play. Special designs to serve as owners' marks should be painted or burned into arrows so that they are easy to identify.

INDIAN DARTS

Plains—Woodland—Northwest Coast

BOYS	3 TO 6 PLAYERS	OUTDOORS
ELEMENTARY—JUNIOR	INDIVIDUAL	

Indian boys threw light darts for accuracy and made a game of who could come closest to various targets in order to see who would count coup. Here is one way in which one of their dart games can be played when there is a fair amount of flat ground available. In a smaller space, the game may be played in an oval, the players going around it the number of times needed.

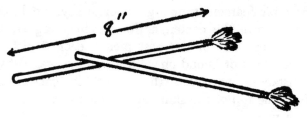

Each player makes three darts. They can be cut from hardwood, or even softwood sticks, so that the finished dart is 8 inches long and tapers from about ¼ inch at one end to ⅜ inch at the other. Instead of taking the trouble to feather the darts as one would an arrow, an easier method may be used by either gluing two fluffy feathers into a hole bored in the center of the ¼-inch end of the dart, or tying two or three feathers onto the thin end. To avoid the probability of serious accidents, such darts should *never* be pointed nor any piece of metal fitted on the end as a point. Naturally all of the darts should be pretty much of the same weight and appearance, to assure fair play for all of the contestants. This is how the contest is carried out.

The first player throws his dart straight ahead and as far as he can. He throws from over the shoulder, holding the dart between the thumb and first two fingers of the throwing hand. The second player throws a dart in an effort to touch the first dart thrown at any point of its length. If his throw is successful, he picks up both his own dart and his opponent's and throws another dart straight forward, from where the two darts lay. The third thrower goes forward to where the second player stands and throws at the second player's dart from there. Should the second player fail to hit the first dart thrown, he leaves both that dart and his own on the ground where they fell, giving the third player a chance to throw, from the starting position, at either of the two darts. If he hits one of the darts on his first throw, he may throw again at the dart not hit. Should he hit both darts in the two throws, he goes forward to where they lie, picks them up and throws another dart from where either lay. Should he hit only one dart on the first throw, and miss the second one, he takes the dart which he struck and his own which struck it, leaving the third dart for the next thrower. The thrower who has all or the most darts at the end of the game is the winner. This version of the game is simplified by having only two players contest, one against the other; and when there are two pairs contesting, the winner of each pair game can compete to decide the champion.

Since various tribes play this dart game in different ways, there is scope for modern chiefs to make their own rules and adaptations.

OKOTOKS

Plains

BOYS   2 TO 9 PLAYERS   OUTDOORS
ELEMENTARY—SENIOR INDIVIDUAL

Blackfoot braves and boys played this game with a big round stone. The modern Indian can play it quite well with a volleyball or basketball. It is played in this way. A line is marked on the ground and a player stands with his back to it, heels just touching the line. He is given a ball and spreads his legs apart, not too far, then throws the ball between them, trying to throw the ball as far as possible before it touches the ground. It takes a certain amount of skill coupled with practice to make the ball travel far when thrown from this position. The distance the ball travels is measured from the line in front of which the thrower stands to the point where the ball first touches the ground.

143

The Indians sometimes have as many as six eager throwers "throw the Okotoks," as they say, from a long line at the same time. Perhaps it is best for modern Indians to throw one at a time and, if the chief so decides, each player may be given three consecutive throws; the score is judged either by the total distance made in all three throws or by the longest of the three throws.

SKY OKOTOKS
Plains

BOYS	2 TO 9 PLAYERS	OUTDOORS
ELEMENTARY—SENIOR	INDIVIDUAL	

While watching some Blackfoot boys "throw the Okotoks" in Alberta the author introduced a fully inflated soccer ball into the game and the boys were well pleased with this new mode of play, chiefly because the ball traveled so much farther than the heavy stones they were using. After a few games played under ceremonial Okotoks rules, the author innovated this new game, which was promptly christened Sky Okotoks, after having the Indian players promise never to play it with stones. In this version of the game, the players, standing in exactly the same position as for the horizontal throw game, contested to see who could throw the ball highest into the air. A chief with a sure eye should give the decisions.

BUMP BALL*
Northwest Coast—Plains

BOYS OR GIRLS	6 TO 12 PLAYERS	OUTDOORS
JUNIOR—SENIOR	TEAM	OR INDOORS

This is an adaptation of a number of games which were played chiefly by Indian boys of the Northwest Coast. They

144

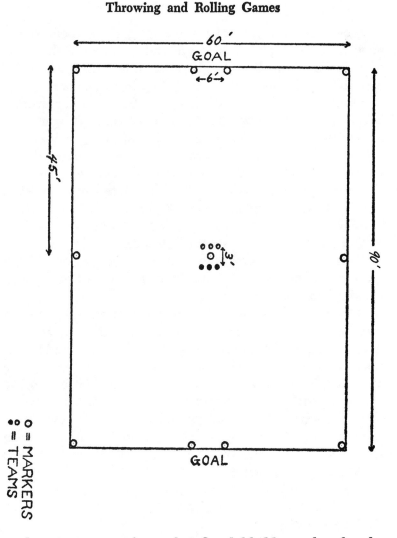

used various sorts of round, inflated bladders taken by the hunters from sea mammals and sometimes covered these bladders with woven fiber nets to protect them against the rough usage they so often received. Some of their games doubtless came from their Eskimo neighbors who kicked, threw, tossed, and drove bladders with whips in many varied games.

Modern Indians can have fun playing Bump Ball, at the same time developing a keen eye and accuracy in throwing. The diagram shows how the play area for this game is laid out. A white ball, or one easily identified by having colored circles or other markings painted on it, is placed on the marker between the two teams. The three players in each team have one brown ball which is passed from player to player or caught by the players on the team as rebounds, either from the driven white ball or the ground, throughout the game. On the word "Play!" each team throws its ball at the white ball in an effort to drive it forward and, eventually, through their opponents' goal. Balls must be thrown, never kicked nor stopped with a foot, and the opposing team's ball must not be thrown by the rival team nor interfered with, except by being struck by the rival team's ball either accidentally or to keep it from driving the white ball forward.

This game can be speeded up by giving each team an extra throwing ball. Considerable skill is required by a team to develop a game which will drive the ball fairly steadily forward, despite the rival team's efforts to drive it in the opposite direction. A good way for a team to develop skill in driving the white ball forward is for each team to line up, facing opposite directions, and drive a ball toward its own goal, without opposition from another team. Indian boys played a form of lone bump ball, by driving one bladder ahead of them by striking it with another.

HIT THE TREE*
Woodland

BOYS OR GIRLS	2 TO 8 PLAYERS	OUTDOORS
ELEMENTARY—SENIOR	INDIVIDUAL—TEAM	OR INDOORS

The Winnebago boys and men played this game to develop their throwing marksmanship. This is understandable, for a well-thrown stone often added a rabbit to the family cooking pot. The players chose a dead tree with a trunk about 8 inches in diameter and threw round stones at it from a distance ranging from 20 to 40 feet. The player who scored the greatest number of hits on the trunk in ten throws was the winner.

A much safer adaptation of this game, which is easier to play and equally good for developing accurate throwing and a strong throwing arm, can be played by modern Indians. The target can be a live tree, since the throwers use a soft rubber ball about the size of a tennis ball. This neither damages the tree nor presents a hazard to players or passers-by. It is good practice, however, for the modern chief to select a dead tree too, should there be one in the vicinity of where the game will be played. The game can be made more difficult and more interesting by marking, with chalk, two lines about 18 inches apart around the side of the tree which is used as a target. The lower line should be marked about 5 feet above ground level. Hitting anywhere within the marked space can be counted as one and a half hits. Players take turn about at throwing, but one who hits within the marked target may be allowed to continue to throw until he misses the tree.

When no suitable tree is to be found nearby, the outline of a tree target can be plainly marked on a wall or fence in the play area. This serves the purpose very well, but the chief must see to it that players never mark either wall or fence without first getting the permission of the director of the play area or the owner of the land on which the game is played. In the latter case, the outline should be carefully rubbed out at the end of the contest.

TOE THROW STICK

Southwest

BOYS OR GIRLS	4 TO 10 PLAYERS	OUTDOORS
ELEMENTARY—SENIOR	INDIVIDUAL—TEAM	

This was a favorite game of the Keres Indians who contested it between teams or individual players. The only equipment needed to stage a contest is a hardwood stick 2 inches long by ¾ inch in diameter and—a bare foot. The latter is not compulsory, but it helps.

A line is marked on the ground and the player stands behind it with the stick balanced on his toes, of either foot. He kicks it upward and forward with a swift, forceful, jerky movement. The player wins whose stick travels the farthest. The point where the stick first strikes the ground decides the distance thrown.

The referee measures the distance made by each kick in order to arrive at his decision. Modern players can play this game well enough while wearing sneakers but the only real way to enjoy it and play really well is barefooted.

FOOT CAST BALL

Southwest

BOYS OR GIRLS	4 TO 10 PLAYERS	OUTDOORS
ELEMENTARY—SENIOR	INDIVIDUAL—TEAM	

Grown-up Indians of the Americas used heavy stones a great deal in their play to show how strong they were. The youngsters copied them by using lighter stones to implement their playways. This game was played to see which player could throw a heavy round stone, balanced on the foot just behind the toes, the farthest. Skill in balancing the stone for the throw, as well as strength for propelling, was required.

An adaptation of this game, offering a safer method of play, can be contested with a basketball or soccer football. The player stands behind a line drawn on the ground and tries to send the ball, balanced as the Indians did, as far as possible. The length of the cast is decided by where the ball first strikes the ground after being thrown from the foot. A little practice can almost double the length of the average player's cast.

DISK ROLL

Northwest Coast

BOYS OR GIRLS	2 TO 10 PLAYERS	OUTDOORS
ELEMENTARY—JUNIOR	INDIVIDUAL	OR INDOORS

A game which the Clatsop youngsters liked was played in this way. Two short thin sticks were forced into the earth, or into a firm, sandy beach, about 12 inches apart. Directly in the middle, between these two uprights, a hole about 3 inches in diameter and depth was made. A line was marked on the ground directly opposite and 10 feet away from this goal and trap. The contestants rolled round, smooth, hardwood disks toward the goal in an endeavor to have each disk roll between the two uprights without being trapped in the hole between them. Each player rolled from three to five disks and the one who got the most disks through the goal in the course of one to five games, as agreed beforehand, won.

Though Indians could play this game, as described, almost anywhere before the white man took over, it is difficult nowadays to find a place in, or even close to, a city or town where even such a small hole can be made in the ground, without violent repercussion, involving the owner of the land, at least! With this in mind, some improvisation is required in order to make Disk Roll suitable for playground and indoor use. Here is how it can be done. Three small, empty matchboxes, or three empty thread spools, can take the place of the goal posts and the hole, while a few checkers complete all of the gear needed. Two of the empty matchboxes are set on the floor 12 inches apart, with the sides of the boxes facing the direction of the line from which the checkers will be rolled. The third matchbox is set up on the floor, in the center and directly between the other two boxes, with the top of the box facing the rolling line. We now have the two goal posts and the hole. The box will serve as a narrower or wider hole acording to how it is placed between the two other boxes. A line is now marked on the floor 10 feet away from the goal, and directly facing it, and the game is ready to roll. The empty spools mentioned may be used in place of the three matchboxes if spools are easier to find. The checkers make fine rolling disks and each player may roll from three to six in succession, as decided by the leader. From 3 to 6 goals may be fixed as the winning score.

STAR BALL*

Northwest Coast

BOYS OR GIRLS	3 TO 9 PLAYERS	OUTDOORS
ELEMENTARY—JUNIOR	INDIVIDUAL	OR INDOORS

On some of the hard, circular, smooth, sandy beaches in front of their villages, youngsters of the Northwest Coast often played games with sand, stones, and round pebbles as the only required equipment. In the Star Game, a player stood in the middle of a star outline, as shown in the diagram. A small round hole about 3 inches in diameter was scooped out in the sand at the points shown in the drawing and the player tried to roll a smooth round pebble, about 2 inches in diameter, into each hole, 15 feet from where he stood with his feet together. The player who succeeded in rolling the most pebbles, in four tries with one aimed at each hole, was the winner and if all four pebbles rolled into the holes, the player had another turn at pebble rolling.

Here is an adaptation of this game which makes it possible to play Star Ball indoors as well as outdoors, without any hole digging. All that is needed are a few tennis balls, or any other sort of rubber ball about that size, and four paper saucers, about 5 inches in diameter and 1 inch deep. A 3½-inch piece is cut out of one side of each saucer, as shown in the diagram.

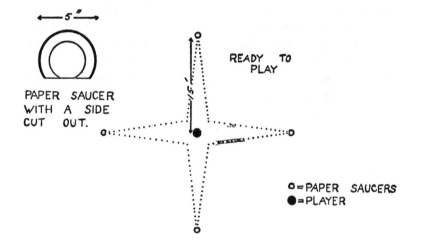

←—5″—→

PAPER SAUCER
WITH A SIDE
CUT OUT.

READY TO
PLAY

o = PAPER SAUCERS
● = PLAYER

When one of these prepared saucers is placed at each of the four points shown in the drawing, the game can be started. If four balls of the right size are not available, each player may roll the same ball four times. The ball must not only roll into the saucer but stay there in order to score. This is perhaps a little more difficult to accomplish than rolling pebbles into sandy holes. The rolling distance is increased as the players' skill increases.

HOLE BALL*

Northwest Coast

BOYS OR GIRLS	3 TO 9 PLAYERS	OUTDOORS
ELEMENTARY—JUNIOR	INDIVIDUAL	OR INDOORS

This is a simplified form of the game which precedes it. It can be played with a ball of about tennis ball size and one cutout saucer. The player bowls at the saucer from a line marked 15 feet distant. The first player to roll three or six balls, as agreed before the game starts, into the saucer is the winner. The rolling distance in this game, as in the preceding one, can be gradually increased as the skill of the players develops.

7.

Games Requiring No Equipment

THE INDIAN YOUNGSTERS played a great number of games without equipment. Quite a few of the games appeared to be complicated or purposeless to an onlooker who had not a fair knowledge at least of games and game patterns. It is for this reason that many of the earliest white travelers and explorers who mentioned Indian games and sports in their reports or diaries frequently wrote, after watching Indian children animatedly playing a game of some sort: "They appeared to be playing some sort of game but it was impossible to determine its purpose." Another reason why it was so difficult for untrained observers to discover the "purpose" of a game was because the players were so skillful and their movements so unbelievably fast that it was almost impossible for the eye to follow them.

The equipment used for so many games was so very simple that almost half of the 150 games in this book could be included in this chapter, were it not for the fact that listing them under other headings makes a better division of play activities for modern leaders and the Indians in their charge.

Place-changing games, in which players moved in fast and intricate formations, were favorites among Indian youngsters. When the author played games such as the one which follows this introduction, with the children of the Northwest Coast, the players would have been surprised by the use of paper, cloth, or even bark markers for many of the games. There were always willing volunteers who enjoyed being human markers, and when they served in that capacity they were as stoic and immobile as though they were inanimate markers. Even the youngest players entered so wholeheartedly into the important role of "markers" that it was often necessary to "collect" them after a game or they were still likely to be standing in the places assigned to them long after a game had ended and another game was in progress nearby. These children never volunteered to be It or a marker with the request that they be allowed to play in the next game. Their philosophical theory was that if they didn't get a chance for more active play that day, then "maybe tomorrow" or some other day their chance would come. Should a modern leader be unable to find suitable human markers for the following place-changing game, it is suggested that he use paper plates instead.

TOUCH AND GO!*

Northwest Coast

| BOYS OR GIRLS | 12 TO 32 PLAYERS | OUTDOORS |
| ELEMENTARY—JUNIOR | TEAM | OR INDOORS |

The two teams playing this game stand in the form of a square cross. The six or eight players on one team stand in one right angle of the cross, while the other team, of the same number of players, stands in the other angle, as shown in the drawing. The distance between the inside player in each line and the marker in the center of the square is 6 feet. The distance between team members is 4 feet. The space between each outside player and the outer marker beside him is 6 feet.

When the chief calls "Change!" the Number 1 player on each team runs around, always outside the two markers, and touches the Number 8 player on the other angle of the team on the shoulder. Any player who moves before he is touched can disqualify his team. Immediately he is touched, he runs around to the place left vacant by player Number 1, touching off player Number 2 in passing. Number 2 player now runs to Number 7's place, and the moves continue in this pattern

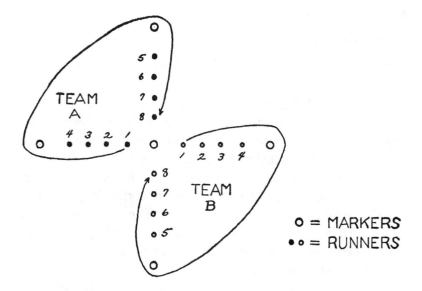

O = MARKERS
•○ = RUNNERS

until each player on each team has changed places with his corresponding player in the opposite arm of the angle. The first team to complete the change is the winner.

When there are thirty-two or more players ready to play at the same time, the chief forms two crosses with an equal number of players in each. In this form of the game, the two teams in each angle not only race against each other, but the angles of each square contest against the angles of the other square, thus deciding *the* champion team of the four. When a simpler form of this relay race is desired for younger players, the team members only race *directly* across the angle, Number 1 to Number 8, and so on.

Though the Indian players frequently criss-crossed in veritable maze patterns in such games, this adaptation is arranged to entirely eliminate the danger of collision.

RING AROUND*

Northwest Coast

BOYS OR GIRLS   12 TO 30 PLAYERS   OUTDOORS
ELEMENTARY—JUNIOR   TEAM

This is one of the "ring-around" games mentioned in Chapter 1. It provided much merriment for girls and boys of all ages. Since the writer had never before seen this game played by children of any tribe, he asked a very old Bella Bella woman if she knew where the game came from. She was not sure, but thought that it was a "gift from the People of the North," meaning, no doubt, the Eskimo. The game needed no equipment and the hardest thing to get in order to play it well, on the extremely rugged Northwest Coast, was sufficient suitable space. Once a level piece of ground was discovered—and the hardy Indian youngsters did not worry about its being too level—the merry game began. Any number of players joined hands and formed two circles, with an equal number of players in each and all players facing toward the center of the circle of which they were a part. In the circle position, each circle raced the other to a tree or rock 100 yards or more distant, which was used as the finish mark. The circle had to be kept formed as the players advanced. The circle which reached the finish mark first, still in a circle and without having lost any players, was the winner. Sometimes each circle had as many as forty players in it and the number of players who fell down, especially among those who ran backward and nearly so, was

156

very great. Falling down was considered part of the fun by these rugged players—the greatest part of it in fact.

To see these boys and girls race as fast as they could and still preserve the shape of the circle, over ground strewn with stones and occasional rocks which had to be avoided, would give any modern leader of games heart failure. On the other hand, playing this game with circles containing not more than a dozen or so players, and on smooth, stone-free ground, provides a lot of fun and is worth trying when it can be carefully supervised. Frequently warning the players that they must always move in the form of a circle in order to win slows the game down nicely.

The writer has played this game with younger Indian players, who did not know how the game was originally played, with the circles so arranged that nearly all players faced the front as they moved forward. This is accomplished by having a circle of say twenty players arranged so that the leading ten players face the finish point, and the other ten players in the rear of the circle also face the finish point. Only a few players may have to run sideways from time to time in such a circle but no player will need to run backward. Older Indian children did not like this form of play because "we do not fall down enough."

It will be found that as a circle moves forward it will nearly always revolve slightly, so that those who are closest to the finish point at the start may be farther away from it at the finish, though one part of the circle has reached the winning mark.

TURTLE KEEPER*
Northwest Coast

BOYS	5 TO 7 PLAYERS	OUTDOORS
ELEMENTARY—JUNIOR	INDIVIDUAL	OR INDOORS

This game is adapted from a game of tag played by some Indian children on the Canadian Northwest Coast, who knew how to play various forms of "safe" tag.

A circle about 30 or 40 feet in diameter is marked on the ground. Five players, representing four turtles and one keeper, take up spread-out positions inside the circle. When a chief shouts "Catch!" the turtle keeper must try to tag all four turtles as quickly as possible. The "catch" is that any turtle is safe who drops to the ground, turns on his back, and raises his arms and legs in air, but he must not remain in that position for longer than the time taken to count 6, slowly. Variations of this game can be played by having the turtle keeper hop on one foot or both feet while tagging, and allowing a turtle who has been tagged to be rescued by being touched by another turtle before he can leave the circle, which he must do as soon as he has been tagged. He must not run toward a free turtle in order to be touched.

OVER AND OVER*
Plains—Southwest—Northwest Coast

BOYS	2 TO 12 PLAYERS	OUTDOORS
ELEMENTARY—JUNIOR	INDIVIDUAL	

There are so many Indian names from all over the Americas for this little game that perhaps the above English title is as suitable as any. Not only Indian children but youngsters all over the world have played this game since man first learned to play. All that was required was a smooth, grassy hillside, ranging from very steep to a gentle slope, to suit all tastes, and the "equipment" was complete. The Seminole of Florida and some tribes of the Canadian Northwest did their downhill roll on steep sand dunes, but that is a rather sandy way which is not recommended for modern Indians.

The author watched some Northwest Coast Indian youngsters play this game in such an original way that it is set down here, not for adoption by modern Indians but because of its general interest. The adaptation that follows it will prove best for modern Indians. These Indian youngsters of the Northwest Coast used a steep, long, smooth, grassy slope and while some rolled down it in any way they pleased, half a dozen played a sort of over-and-on relay that was very amusing to watch. Some of the players who did not know how to flatten out at the right moment got considerably bumped, which they seemed to think only added to the fun. An older boy was in charge and he showed them their positions. One player was stationed at the very top of the steep slope, ready to roll. Another boy was directly in line and below him on the hill about 50 feet below. Fifty feet below him was another roller. When the big boy gave a shrill call, which was the "Go!" signal, the player on top of the hill rolled directly down onto and entirely over the second player, after which the first player swung around, feet pointing downhill, and abruptly stopped. The second player, unperturbed by the rude way of being touched off, was on his way in a flash, until he rolled swiftly against the third player, who continued the fast roll to the foot of the hill. Once he arrived there, the other two players rolled down and joined him in the climb up for another fast downhill roll.

These Indian boys wore a combination breech-clout-shorts and were barefoot. The lower layers of players lay on their stomachs, with shoulders and hips slightly tilted toward the oncoming roller, and each kept his face turned toward him until he was only about 10 feet away, then promptly turned it in the other direction. With their bodies held as they did, the oncoming roller quite often rolled completely over them at top speed. They played for some time and then a rival team of three boys, an older boy-leader, some substitutes and on-lookers, arrived. The boys of both teams were arranged in two lanes, about 10 feet apart, which did not allow much leeway for an angle roller. On the signal, the first roller on each team shot downhill and the roll-relay was underway. Both teams won once and it took a third roll to determine the one which had the right to count coup.

Here is an adaptation of their game for modern Indians who have a roomy, suitable, and not too steep hill somewhere within their play area. In order to avoid a roller from getting a bare foot on the back of the head, modern Indians should be given just three times as much space, to eliminate chance of collision—which the Northwest players regarded as the best means of touch-off. Instead of lining the three or four partici-pants in each team in a straight line, the modern chief arranges them so that no roller can roll into another. He does this by allowing 12 feet between the rollers in each team and a 20-foot lane between teams. The rollers in the downhill positions are told that each must start to roll just as soon as the boy who is to start him off, by remote control, arrives in line with him. Being in no danger from swifty revolving feet or head, the boy to be touched off will be able to watch closely and to start at the exact moment when the roller from uphill is exactly in line with him. Once a player has touched off another, in the way described, he should wait until the roller ahead of him has reached the finish line at the foot of the hill before starting his own descent.

The only difficulty for modern chiefs in carrying out this amusing relay is to find a safe, suitable hill with a sloping face wide enough to accommodate the rather far-spread rollers. A sloping hill face of 100 feet will accommodate two teams of rollers.

HOP!

Plains—Woodland—Northwest Coast

BOYS OR GIRLS   4 TO 16 PLAYERS   OUTDOORS

ELEMENTARY—JUNIOR   INDIVIDUAL   OR INDOORS

The Indian youngsters had just as good a time playing games as we have today, though they either played games which required no equipment or played with the simple things provided by nature and fashioned for use in games by themselves or parents. Three simple games follow which require no equipment at all.

From just behind a straight line marked on the ground, Indian children played Hop! by racing to another line marked on the ground from 30 to 60 feet distant. They used three methods of hopping which we can copy: hop race on the right foot only, hop race on the left foot only, and hop race on both feet with the feet held close together. Indian game leaders often made such games more interesting and exciting by having the older players hop two or three times between the two lines: the first time on the left foot, the return on the right foot, and the final hop with both feet together as they raced for the third time between the two lines. The player who came in first and had hopped in the right order throughout the race was the one who counted coup and won. Modern leaders can add a little to this race by having the hoppers hold up the right or left foot while hopping. This additional touch seems to throw many players off balance, which adds to the fun of the game.

HOP, JUMP!

Plains—Woodland—Northwest Coast

BOYS OR GIRLS   4 TO 16 PLAYERS   OUTDOORS

ELEMENTARY—JUNIOR   INDIVIDUAL   OR INDOORS

This race is different from the one which precedes it, since between hops, a jump for as long a distance as possible was made with both feet together or with one foot thrust ahead of the other, as decided by the leader before the race. Of course all players had to do the same thing in order to hop jump a fair race.

The distance between the two lines ranged from 40 to 80 feet and even farther for older players. The players could hop on either the right or left foot before making the jump. It was hard to make good time in this race because it was difficult to change from hop to jump and jump to hop without stumbling or stopping. A player who stumbled or fell had to hop back three hops before he could start again. The timing throughout this race was hop, jump; hop, jump; hop, jump, and that is how modern Indians can run this race today.

HOP BETWEEN!

Plains—Woodland—Northwest Coast

BOYS OR GIRLS   4 TO 16 PLAYERS   OUTDOORS

ELEMENTARY—JUNIOR   INDIVIDUAL   OR INDOORS

This was another version of the Hop, Jump! race in which the jump had to be made before and after each hop. The jump, as in the former race, could be taken with both feet held closely together or with one foot traveling ahead of the other but, of course, the style of jumping was decided by the chief before the race started. This made the race fair for all contestants. The timing for this race was jump, hop, jump; jump, hop, jump, which many players found hard to do. In order to vary this race a chief often had the first race contested with both feet held together for the jumps, while in the second race the players jumped with one foot thrust out ahead of the other. Players will have to try these racing ways to find out how difficult it is to keep balanced and travel forward from jump to hop.

Players who lose balance or get mixed up in the correct sequence of the jumps and hops can be dropped from the race by the chief, or may continue to the end without being able to count coup, or in other words, win. The Indians invariably disqualified all players who failed in a game in any way, in order that the youngsters might learn the correct way to do things, even under stress. Such an idea is just as fair and practical today as it was then.

JUMP RACE*

Plains—Woodland—Northwest Coast

BOYS OR GIRLS	4 TO 16 PLAYERS	OUTDOORS
ELEMENTARY—JUNIOR	INDIVIDUAL	OR INDOORS

The Indian children liked jumping, and jump races of many kinds were common. At times they raced in rabbit-hop style and a race in bear style will be found in this book. When these youngsters tired of animal-mimicry races, and it took them a very long time to tire of anything, they devised jumping games in which they jumped forward, sideways, and back. It is because of the danger in jumping backward that this safe, tricky, and amusing adaptation of two of the Indian jumping games has been devised.

The racers line up 4 feet apart just behind a line drawn on the ground and facing another line 60 feet distant. The jumpers are told by the chief that they must jump, with their feet held close together, in this order: *first,* jump to left; *second,* jump to right; *third,* jump forward as far as possible. There is nothing tricky about this arrangement so, after these three jumps, which must be done in correct sequence, the order changes in the next group of jumps and it is right, left, then forward. The next series of jumps follows the first pattern and so on until the finish line is reached. A jumper who jumps in a wrong pattern must turn around and take three long jumps toward the starting line, as a penalty, before continuing the race. The first jumper who reaches the finish line and has carried out the correct jump patterns from the start of the race, or has penalized himself for all faults made since the start of the race, counts coup and wins.

Chiefs will find the patterns still more difficult if they ask the jumpers to do each pattern twice, or three times, in succession. In this form of the race the jumpers become used to the first pattern, having done it twice or three times, and find it harder to change into the new jump pattern in consequence. This race can also be carried out as a relay race, with two or three jumpers, on the same team, starting out from the finish line, when touched off, in addition to the two or three at the starting line.

CROOKED PATH

Plains—Woodland—Northwest Coast

BOYS AND GIRLS 6 TO 18 PLAYERS OUTDOORS
ELEMENTARY INDIVIDUAL

Follow My Leader, known as Crooked Path to some Plains tribes, was played by many Indian tribes throughout the United States and Canada by groups of boys, girls, and mixed groups of boys and girls. The player chosen as leader sang a simple, rhythmic song, sometimes made up on the spot, as he led the line of players. For instance, a translation of one of the Plains' tribes Crooked Path songs is: *Follow the leader, follow him well, what he'll do next, no one can tell.*

As the leader walked or ran ahead of the other players, who followed him in Indian file, he made any steps, jumps, or motions that occurred to him. At times he imitated the movements of birds or beasts and performed dance steps to make it difficult for the other players to follow him correctly. All who failed to do so dropped out of the line. When all or nearly all were out, a new game with a new leader began. Sometimes the game took the form of a prank game in which the file of players pranced through the village, playing jokes on the occupants of tipi or longhouse as they went.

The Indian youngsters always played this game with a lilt and sense of rhythm, since most of the movements were made in time to the simple tune being sung, or even hummed, by the leader.

TURNABOUT

Northwest Coast

BOYS OR GIRLS	4 TO 16 PLAYERS	OUTDOORS
ELEMENTARY—JUNIOR	INDIVIDUAL	

This little game, which helps to develop balance, was played by both girls and boys, and grownups too. A great many of these Indian players moved with a precision and lightness which had to be seen to be believed.

All of the players stood in a straight line or circle with about 3 feet between the players. When the leader who directed the game, without participating, called "Jump one!" the players sprang into the air with their legs held close together and, without bending their knees, jumped clockwise one quarter circle. On "Jump two!" another quarter circle leap was made, and so on until each player, after four jumps, was back in his original position, facing front again.

On the second time around, the "Jump one!" command was the signal for the players to jump one half circle, so that two jumps took them round to the front again.

The last jump was hardest of all. When the chief called "Big Jump!" each player made a spinning leap clockwise into the air, whirling completely around so that he landed facing the front and without any movement after he landed.

The arms were never used when making these jumps and the legs were hardly bent at the knees. Even during the big jump, the entire body spun in a straight, graceful line. Jumpers who landed clumsily or moved their feet or body after they landed were dropped from the game after the first or second mistake was made.

Modern chiefs can experiment with this little jumping game by having the players spin in the counterclockwise direction, which many jumpers find more difficult than the spin to the right. They can also introduce a three-quarter and then a quarter turn in preparation for the "Big Jump!" Half-circle jumps can also be alternated with quarter-circle ones.

LOG SIT*

Woodland

BOYS OR GIRLS	4 TO 12 PLAYERS	OUTDOORS
ELEMENTARY—JUNIOR	TEAM	

The author devised this outdoor "counting out" method game after hearing a Woodland chief tell this little parable:

"A white chief sat on a big long log beside an Indian chief. Suddenly, the white chief said, 'I haven't enough room—move over a little.' The Indian did not see how the white man could be crowded, as they both sat on the middle of the log, but he moved over a little to oblige the white man. Soon the Indian felt the white man push against him, and again ask for more room. Once more the Indian moved over. The white man kept up his tactics until the Indian could move no further and he fell off the end of the log to the ground."

The modern Indians can "count out" in this way, provided there is a long log nearby. The first player on either of the two teams sits on one end of the log. A player from the other team then sits close beside him. This alternate seating arrangement continues until a player from one of the teams finds that there is no room left for him to sit on the log. His team loses the toss. The last player to sit down must have enough room to actually sit on the log and neither overhang it nor half-sit on his neighbor. An alert chief may win the toss for his side by saving his thinnest player for an emergency, unless a still more alert chief uses his stoutest player to checkmate even the thinnest player's seathold.

TILLIKUM!*

Northwest Coast

BOYS OR GIRLS   2 TO 14 PLAYERS   OUTDOORS

ELEMENTARY—JUNIOR   INDIVIDUAL—TEAM   OR INDOORS

Tillikum is a Chinook word meaning "friend." It is played in almost the same way as the Japanese game known as *Jankempo*, which was probably played by the Indian boys and girls of the Northwest Coast in ages past, soon after they came from Asia. The game may be played by two players or contested by two teams. This form of the game makes use of the three elements—Earth, Water, and Fire—and signs are used in playing the game.

This is how the signs are made:

> *Earth* is indicated by holding the right hand out flat, palm downward.
>
> *Water* is shown by letting the fingers and thumb hang downward, with the back of the hand facing forward, to indicate falling water.
>
> *Fire* is illustrated by raising the fingers and thumb, like fingers of mounting fire, with the fingers and thumb pointing upward and the palm of the hand facing forward.

All of these signs are made by one hand, with the arm outstretched and the hand held just above waist level.

The scoring is done in this way:

> *Earth* drinks the *Water,* and wins.
> *Water* puts out the *Fire,* and wins.
> *Fire* scorches the *Earth,* and wins.

Each two players or teams face each other in parallel lines, 2 paces apart, holding their right hands closed and at waist level, wrist held close to waist. On the word "Go!" which can be given by a chief, the players bring their clenched fists from waist level up to shoulder level, then down to waist level again, three times. To regulate the speed of these motions, as uniform time must be kept, each player says aloud, *Til-Li* in two distinct syllables, as the closed hand is raised rather slowly from waist to shoulder level, and *Kum!* as the closed hand is brought swiftly down to waist level again. Each player must keep time with his opponent, and open his right hand, outstretched and at waist level, at the same moment as his rival on the third syllable *Kum!*—making one of any of the three signs which he has chosen. The signs made decide the winner, as explained in the scoring rules.

When two players make the same sign, and this may happen fairly frequently, the result is a tie and the players try again. The winner is best decided by the result of three tries, not counting ties.

When two teams are contesting, each team stands behind a straight line marked on the ground, facing the other team, with a distance of 2 paces between teams. Each team chooses its team captain, who decides on the sign he wishes his team to make and shows it secretly to the members. The teams stand back to back while the sign is being decided on and shown to the team members, after which the teams face each other and are ready to begin. Time is kept best when the team captains take turns at calling out the three syllables, while themselves keeping time, so that the members of both teams work in unison.

8.

Skill Games

PEBBLE PICTURES
Plains

| BOYS AND GIRLS | 2 TO 8 PLAYERS | OUTDOORS |
| ELEMENTARY—SENIOR | INDIVIDUAL | OR INDOORS |

The children of some of the Indian tribes could draw pictures on the sand quite skillfully and some used varicolored sands to make colorful designs. Perhaps some wise old Teton chief watched a raccoon sorting and arranging round pebbles on the bank of a stream one fine morning of Indian summer and that is how pebble pictures reached the children of that tribe. The Teton, among other tribes, encouraged artistic talent among the children, and they held contests in which the youngsters made outlines in pebbles of animals, trees, birds, stars, and tipis, among many other things. The earth was flattened out and then each contestant was given eighteen pebbles, usually white, which they placed on the ground in any formation they desired. A chief judged the contest and the youngster who made the best pebble picture was the winner. Modern Indians can use pebbles of different colors or colored wooden beads for their contests.

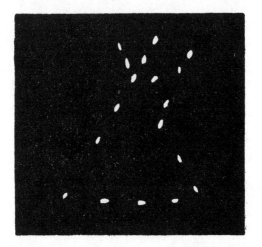

BIRD FLIGHT

Plains—Woodland—Northwest Coast—Southwest

BOYS OR GIRLS	2 TO 6 PLAYERS	OUTDOORS
ELEMENTARY—SENIOR	INDIVIDUAL—TEAM	OR INDOORS

This game, which is still popular in many countries under the name of Battledore and Shuttlecock, was played long, long ago with crude, improvised equipment by the Indian children of the Americas. Some players struck the "bird" with the palms of either or both hands, while many others used an effective "bat" made of thin slats of wood. These bats measured about 13 by 11 inches, with a handle ranging from 5 to 7 inches attached to the back of the bat. Some bats were round, others were square. The "shuttlecock" was made from a piece of very light wood, carved so that there was a heavy and light end, and two or three fluffy feathers were stuck into the lighter end. A light twig, feathered at the lighter end, was used by some tribes, while little bundles of dried corn husks with two or

172

three light, fluffy feathers tied to the top of the bundle made a very good shuttlecock for other tribes.

Modern Indians can use any one of the round wooden bats available these days, unless they want to have the fun of making a bat, and the shuttlecock can easily be made from a big light cork with two or three light feathers stuck in the small end of it. Players bat the "bird" to each other, as in tennis, but a net is not needed.

SNOW BOAT
Woodland

BOYS   2 TO 6 PLAYERS   OUTDOORS
JUNIOR—SENIOR   INDIVIDUAL

Both men and boys of the Seneca and other Woodland tribes liked to compete in the game of Snow Boat. The main factor in the game, bountifully supplied by nature, was snow and crisp, cold weather. The Indians used a hardwood model of a canoe, about 16 inches long, with a white, often fluffy, feather stuck in the stern. The Indian carvers of these "racing" canoes left as much solid wood inside the craft as possible in order to increase the weight of the completed canoe. They slid these snow boats down special runways, built like a straight trench down a steep, snow-covered hill. Sometimes, though seldom, the boats were slid down a smooth, ice-covered hillside. The

bottoms of these boats were coated with ice just before the race so that they were ready for swift descent down the hill.

Some races were begun by each contestant giving his canoe a push-off when the "Go!" signal was given, but usually the canoes were simply placed at the head of a snow boat run and allowed to start off on their own, traveling faster and faster as they gained way, so that when they reached the foot of the hill their momentum carried them far out over the flat snow-covered or icy plain at the foot of the slope. The winner of this race was either the one whose boat traveled the farthest or the one whose craft traveled the fastest, according to the arrangement made before the race took place.

BALL IN AIR

Northwest Coast—Plains

| BOYS OR GIRLS | 2 TO 6 PLAYERS | OUTDOORS |
| JUNIOR—SENIOR | INDIVIDUAL | OR INDOORS |

This type of captive ball game was played by the women of many tribes. They kept a fairly soft ball, attached to a 24-inch thong, in the air by kicking it with either foot while holding the other end of the thong in one hand. The balls were made from almost any soft material packed inside a buckskin cover, or the intestines of sea mammals, well-inflated and sometimes covered with a woven net to add strength, were used. These balls measured from 7½ to 12½ inches in diameter and the length of the thong varied somewhat, 2 feet being the usual length, though sometimes it was a foot longer. One ball is required for each player.

The women were exceedingly skillful in keeping the ball continuously in the air, even when they kicked it hard—as most of them did. Just as soon as the thong jerked the ball back or down, a toe was ready to contact the ball and send it up again. The game was played while standing almost on the same spot, but a player was not disqualified who moved around in a rather small circle. One miss and out was the rigid rule. The Cheyenne women played this game with an elliptical ball which measured about 7½ inches in diameter.

Boys who play soccer will find this game good fun and not at all easy.

Modern Indians can use a volleyball, with the thong tied to the laces, or balloons of various sizes, for this game.

CAPTIVE BALL

Northwest Coast

GIRLS OR BOYS	2 TO 6 PLAYERS	OUTDOORS
JUNIOR–SENIOR	INDIVIDUAL	OR INDOORS

This game is played with exactly the same equipment used for Ball in Air. To play this game, the hand is used as a bat to keep the ball in air. As played by most tribes, the hand which held the end of the thong attached to the ball could not be used as the striking hand. Women generally played this fast game and contested one against the other. Each started to keep her ball in the air at the same moment, and the one who first missed the ball was the loser. The ball was struck with surprising force, and a good player never seemed to try to work out easy rebounds but was ready to strike the ball as it bounced back from any point or angle.

As in the former game, modern Indians may use volleyballs or balloons to play this game.

BALL JUGGLE RACE
Plains—Southwest

GIRLS	2 TO 8 PLAYERS	OUTDOORS
JUNIOR—SENIOR	INDIVIDUAL	OR INDOORS

The Shoshone and Ute women were especially good at this juggling game, generally known as *Tapa*. They played it by juggling two or three, rarely four, gypsum balls in the air, keeping them in almost constant flight as they walked or ran toward some fixed point, such as a rock, tree, or tipi. The first player to arrive at the chosen mark was the winner, provided she had not dropped a ball, failed to keep all of them in motion, or tripped en route from the starting point to the goal. Sometimes rounded lightweight stones were used, and the Indian women of New Mexico used hard, stuffed, cloth-covered balls about 6 inches in diameter for the game.

It is easy for the modern Indian girl to play this game, using tennis or any other rubber balls, not exceeding 6 inches in diameter, and certainly not attempting to juggle more than two balls at a time until considerable skill has been developed in tossing and catching the balls while walking in a fixed direction.

This race should only be carried out on smooth level ground that has been thoroughly combed for stones or other obstructions prior to the event. Any uneven ground is unsuitable for this race, as a twisted ankle could be the result of trying to walk or run with the eyes turned skyward.

DROP STICK

Northwest Coast

BOYS OR GIRLS	3 TO 12 PLAYERS	OUTDOORS
ELEMENTARY—JUNIOR	INDIVIDUAL	OR INDOORS

This game, a favorite of the Kwakiutl and other Northwest Coast tribes, requires more skill than equipment. A ring 2½ inches in diameter made from whalebone was tied onto the thick end of a pointed stick 24 inches long, the stick being tied on outside the ring. A pliable twig or withe sometimes took the place of the bone ring. Twenty-four plain straight sticks 8¾ inches long and about ¼ inch in diameter completed

the gear. The pointed end of the stick with the ring was thrust into the ground for about 4 inches, and a player was given the twenty-four sticks. He stood beside the ring stick and tried, with either hand, to drop the sticks, one by one, and from shoulder level, through the ring onto the ground. One player kept track of the score of each player, and all had a turn at dropping the sticks.

Some players became so skillful at this game that they quickly dropped the entire twenty-four sticks through the ring, one by one, without a miss. There was a more difficult form of the game for such expert players—it was played blindfolded. If a player became too adept in this version of the game also he was, while blindfolded, whirled around a few times and then, while the amused onlookers kept perfectly quiet, tried to drop the sticks through the ring. Quite often he did!

Modern Indians can make this game very easily by using round dowel sticks and a piece of thick wire to form the ring on the ring stick. Only half the number of sticks can be dropped by each player, should the chief so decide.

BALL DROP

Northwest Coast

BOYS OR GIRLS	3 TO 12 PLAYERS	OUTDOORS
ELEMENTARY—JUNIOR	INDIVIDUAL	OR INDOORS

Even less equipment was required for this game than for Drop Stick. Both boys and girls played it by dropping a small ball cut from a piece of softwood, a pebble, or a bead into a sea shell measuring about 5 inches in diameter and 3 inches deep. The ball, bead, or pebble measured about 1 inch in diameter.

This game was played in the same way as Drop Stick. The players stood beside the shell and, from shoulder level with the hand held at arm's length, tried to drop the object decided on into the shell so that it would remain inside.

Each player had three tries; only the ball, bead, or twig that fell into and remained in the shell scored—those which bounced out did not count. When players became too good at this game when played in the manner described, they then played it blindfolded, or by turning around fast, once or more times, prior to dropping the ball.

Modern Indians can play this game by using small paper or sponge rubber balls, measuring about 1 inch in diameter, and dropping them into a deep paper cup or container, or a bowl of some sort that is not too wide across the rim.

Skill Games

RING IN A RING
Southwest

BOYS OR GIRLS	4 TO 10 PLAYERS	OUTDOORS
ELEMENTARY—JUNIOR	INDIVIDUAL—TEAM	OR INDOORS

The Pueblo People were fond of this game which the Zuni boys called *Tsi-ko-Wai*. This is how they played. Two rings were made from flexible smooth twigs. One ring measured 3½ inches in diameter, while the other was 2¾ inches in diameter. The biggest ring was wrapped in alternate quarters with blue yarn for one quarter and green yarn for the next, which made two blue and two green quarters in the circle. The smaller ring was wrapped around with white yarn. The rings were wrapped in this fashion simply on account of the Indian love for decoration and color.

The big ring was placed on the ground and the small ring was tossed from a distance of 10 to 20 feet, the object being to place it directly inside the big ring without touching any part of it with the smaller ring. The winner was sometimes decided by the best score in three or six throws, but often the games went on for a long time until the winner was clearly indicated by the result of the many games contested.

BEAVER LODGE
Northwest Coast—Plains—Woodland

BOYS OR GIRLS	2 TO 6 PLAYERS	OUTDOORS
ELEMENTARY—JUNIOR	INDIVIDUAL	OR INDOORS

This is an old Indian game which one easily recognizes as Jack Straws. Indian children played it with straws, long stalks of heavy grass, thin reeds, and thin straight twigs, thrown in a loose pile on the ground. This loosely piled mound of reeds or twigs looked like a miniature beaver lodge, and because of this likeness the author chose Beaver Lodge as a title for this

179

game instead of using the native name. The Indian youngsters did not use a hook to remove the pile of straws, one by one, while attempting to do so without disturbing those not being removed at that moment. Instead, they used the thumb and forefinger of one hand only, or, occasionally, two straight slender sticks about 15 inches long, one held in each hand. The rules were simple and can be adopted by modern Indians. If a straw or reed was dropped, once it had been picked up clear of the others, the player who dropped it was ruled out of that game. If a reed was displaced while the pile was being dismantled, the player responsible was disqualified. The winner was the player who removed the greatest number of reeds successfully.

The number of straws or reeds used in this game differed greatly. At least thirty seemed to be the average number but sometimes Indian players, with their remarkable patience to sustain them, would cheerfully tackle a pile of a hundred or more reeds.

There were a number of ways in which this game was played. Usually one pile of straws, or similar material, was picked apart by one player. Often three players were busy with their own piles of straws at the same time. Occasionally two or three players worked on one pile and, rarely, half a dozen players tackled a really big pile of reeds or twigs, all players working at the same time. These Indian children, when they dropped or disturbed a reed, disqualified themselves!

DOUBLE BALL

Plains—Southwest

GIRLS	8 TO 12 PLAYERS	OUTDOORS
SENIOR	TEAM	

The women of many Indian tribes played the game of Double Ball. It was practically never played by men, with the exception of a few California tribes. The double balls and tossing sticks varied, and either regular goals of varying widths between goal posts were used or a post at each end of the playing field served as goals. In the case of regular goals, the double ball had to be hung by the short thong or cord, joining the two balls, over a crossbar in order to score a goal. This method of scoring took very considerable skill, even without the fierce opposition the players encountered before reaching

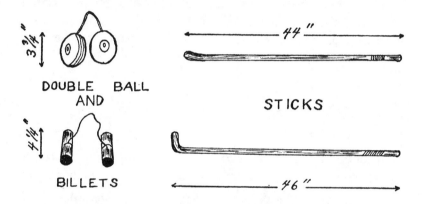

DOUBLE BALL AND BILLETS

STICKS

the rival team's goal. The Pima women, of Arizona, played this game on a smooth 400-yard stretch of terrain. They used willow or alder tossing sticks, about 45 inches long and slightly curved at the thinner end, in order to make it easier to pick up the ball by the thong. These sticks tapered from about 1½ inches thick to about ¾ inch. The double ball used by the Pima women, unlike many others, was an easily made affair formed by knotting a stout leather thong a number of times at each end so that there was a 6-inch, 4-strand, 2-ply leather thong connecting the two knotted balls. It was under this thong that they hooked their sticks and made terrific throws of unbelievable distances. Some tribes used balls stuffed with hair and covered with buckskin, while others played with two wooden billets

4¼ inches long, joined by a strong thong about 7 or 8 inches in length, as shown in the drawings.

While the author is in favor of using the double ball for races over varying distances, he is not keen on Double Ball as a team game because of the considerable risk of players being poked in the eye by sticks of the rival team. As the opposing teams race at top speed toward each other in an effort to pick up the double ball from the ground by thrusting a stick under its thong, it is much easier for a chief to tell the players to keep their sticks pointing downward at all times than for the excited players to obey his instructions. This game is recorded because it was a representative Indian game, but because of the risks mentioned it is *not recommended* for modern players.

DART AND RINGS*

Southwest

| BOYS OR GIRLS | 3 TO 6 PLAYERS | INDOORS |
| ELEMENTARY—JUNIOR | INDIVIDUAL | OR OUTDOORS |

This is one of the very many games of this sort played by the Indians of the Americas from Coast to Coast. The game was selected for this book because it is easily made, easily modified to suit players of all ages, and is not nearly as difficult as many of the other games of a similar kind. Let us see how it was played by the women and children of the Indians of the Southwest.

A smooth stick about 9 inches long and ½ inch thick, slightly pointed at one end, was the "dart." Rings cut from gourds, 1½ to 5 inches in diameter, and numbering from four to as many as eight were strung, like beads, on a 20-inch length of thin woven string, one end of which was fastened to the stick about ¾ inch from the top. So that the rings cut from the gourd did not fall off the end of the string, the end of a gourd was fastened to the end of the twine on which the rings rested. The player swung the rings upward and as many as possible were speared on the stick as they fell. When a player tried and failed to catch one or more rings, as agreed in advance, she handed the dart and rings over to her opponent who then took her turn.

As gourds growing wild are not found in many parts of the United States, a little improvisation will have to be done in order to make the game possible in the gourdless sections of the country. The stick is easily made from a dowel stick, and strong thin twine will serve nicely as the cord, so the only thing that remains to be made is the rings. They can be made from strong, supple cardboard, with the cutout rings ranging in diameter from 1½ to 5 inches and the rims of all the rings being about ⅜ inch in width. The number of rings can be from four to six, half of them being large and the other half small, threaded onto the string in the order of one large, then one small ring. The rings can be held in place on the cord, once one end is securely attached to the top of the stick about 1 inch from the top, by simply tying a circle of thin cardboard to the lower end of the twine.

Modern Indians can take turn about or, when several dart and ring sets are made, compete one against the other, each using his or her own set. Scoring can be counted on a basis of 1 point for each large ring caught on the dart and 3 points for each little ring caught at each throw.

STICK AND RING

Plains—Woodland—Northwest Coast

BOYS OR GIRLS	3 TO 6 PLAYERS	INDOORS
ELEMENTARY—JUNIOR	INDIVIDUAL	OR OUTDOORS

This is the simplest of all ring-tossing games. Merely by using smaller or larger rings, to suit the skill of the various players, this game can be made suitable for players of all ages.

Many grown-up Indians spent a lot of time in perfecting themselves in the art of consistently catching the smallest ring possible, in the belief that the game provided training for the eye. The Eskimo were past masters at this game.

Here is the simple equipment required: a piece of round dowel stick from 10 to 12 inches long and ½ inch in diameter; a length of strong, smooth, thin twine about 16 or 18 inches long; and three or four light metal or bone rings measuring from ¾ to 2 inches in diameter. One ring of the desired size is tied onto one end of the twine, and the other end is tied onto the stick after the end has been slightly pointed about ¾ inch from the top. The lower end of the stick is held in one hand, with the ring hanging down on the end of the twine. The ring is then jerked or swung up as smoothly as possible and the player tries to spear it with the end of the stick so that the ring encircles the stick. The player waits until the ring goes above the end of the stick and tries to spear it as it falls.

It is suggested that this little contest be carried out on the best-out-of-three-tries basis for each contestant. It is more fun when each of two or three players has a stick and ring of his own so that they may all compete at the same time, each using the same size ring. As a player's skill develops, he decreases the size of the ring used.

A number of tribes fastened the twine a third of the way up from the lower end of the stick.

RACKET BALL
Plains—Woodland

BOYS   12 TO 24 PLAYERS   OUTDOORS
JUNIOR—SENIOR   TEAM

This game, from which modern Indians get the game of lacrosse, was played by many tribes, though different types of rackets and various size balls were used. The game was almost exclusively played by men, though it was a favorite game of both men and women of the warlike Winnebago. The men of that tribe used a racket but the women played what was considered the same game, using a double ball and a straight stick. The difference in the rackets used was considerable, as the drawings of the various sorts used by Plains and Woodland tribes illustrate. The circle of the rackets varied from the small, shallow, netted cup measuring about 4 inches in diameter, to

WOODLAND

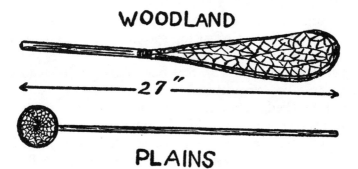

PLAINS

the long, oval cup about 18 inches in length and shaped as shown in the sketch. This type of stick was favored by the Iroquoian tribes, and the modern lacrosse racket is modeled in that pattern. All of the cups in which the balls were carried were netted by a rather closely woven net being fastened on securely to the rim. The sticks did not vary greatly in length, the majority being about 26 or 27 inches in over-all length. Various types of goals were used, ranging from single posts, such as used by the Chippewa, of varying thickness and heights, to two goal posts set at various distances apart to form regular goals. The length of the field on which Racket Ball was played varied from 25 to 50 yards or more. The teams were also composed of varying numbers of players from six on a side to as many players as the field would accommodate. The goal posts, a stick for each player, and a ball for the two teams contesting were the only equipment needed. The balls used, usually hair-stuffed buckskin-covered ones, measured from 2½ to 3 inches in diameter. This is how the Indians played the game, frequently with considerable ceremony.

The two teams were arranged in almost any formation between their own goals and the center of the field. The referee threw the ball from center field high and straight up into the air, then got out swiftly from under as the players from both sides made a wild rush for the ball as it fell, trying to get their rackets under it before it hit the ground. The player catching the ball in his net set off at top speed, dodging and weaving to avoid rival players who charged him in order to try to knock the ball from his racket so that one of their side could gain possession of it. When the player carrying the ball was hard pressed, he tried, before it was too late, to throw the ball to one of his own side who might be running alongside but still far enough away, as a rule, to be able to slip swiftly away from the rival team's players just as soon as he had the ball in his net.

Though the players pursuing the one carrying the ball were supposed to try and strike his stick sharply upward so that the ball was dislodged from the net, this was a difficult thing to do in the speed and excitement of the game. Free-for-all fights frequently developed as the result of players being struck, accidentally or otherwise, on the head or arms. The Guardian of the Goal tried to prevent the player carrying the ball from scoring. When he succeeded, he sent the ball flying back into the field, passing it to a teammate when not too hard pressed to do so. The referee had always to be close to the goal to which the ball was being carried in order to decide that a goal had or had not been scored. When a goal was scored he took the ball to center field and tossed it up in order to start the game again. In the Indian form of the game there were few rules and only rare declaration of fouls. When a player was knocked out, another one, from the reserves on his side, took his place.

Older modern Indians can have fun and exercise playing this game, for which the simple equipment required can easily be made. The goals can be made from poles about 2 inches in diameter, 7 feet long, and driven into the ground 3 feet. The goal posts can be from 4 to 6 feet apart. Single goal posts require too much skill in scoring for beginners. A tennis or similar ball can be used and the rackets made from supple saplings, tapering from a diameter of about 1½ inches to about ¾ inch at the thinner end. The over-all length of the racket should be 32 inches, with the thinner end shaved fairly flat so that when it is bent over to lash onto the straight part of the handle, it can easily be attached securely with strong waxed cord. A piece of netting of almost any sort, provided it is not too stiff, can be attached to the rim with a piece of strong twine, so that it hangs down inside for about 2½ inches at the deepest part. Apart from the ownership mark, painted or burned onto the handle, the racket is now complete. The Iroquoian shape of racket is the best for modern Indians. The length of the field can be around 50 yards, or less when the confines of civilization have imposed drastic limits, and it need not be more than 20 yards in width. Three or more goals can be set as the number to decide which team counts coup. The game should be played carefully and sportingly with a chief to supervise play and act as referee.

TURN STICK

Woodland—Northwest Coast

BOYS   3 TO 6 PLAYERS   OUTDOORS
ELEMENTARY—JUNIOR   INDIVIDUAL

Often when an Indian boy found or cut a nice straight stick he asked himself the question, "What can I best do with it so that I can play a game by myself or with the other boys?" He experimented until he found many answers to his question. Here is one of them. With a stick about 3 feet long and from ½ to 1 inch thick, with a bright stripe painted around one end, he played a game which he called Turn Stick. He found that with practice he could play the game well enough to challenge his friends. They contested in this way.

Each boy took turns. The first boy held the stick in one hand by the end which was not painted. He held the stick a little way out in front of him and threw it gently up so that it made one half turn in the air, falling with the painted stripe toward him. After each boy had a turn at doing this, the first boy then threw the stick up so that it made one complete turn in the air, landing with the painted end pointing away from him.

When it came to his turn again he threw the stick for one and a half turns, then two, then three, and the winner was the player who made his stick turn, in correct sequence, the greatest number of times in the air. The player would call out, "Three turns, make I," so that there was no doubt as to what he intended to make the stick do. Sometimes he spoke to the stick and explained just what he expected it to do. Many players believed that this helped. Some held the stick up to each of the Four Winds before making a difficult throw and when the throw was successful the player gave thanks to the Four Winds for his coup. One significant thing has not been told about this game. Some very important things were required to decide who was the winner. These things were: keen, quick, observant Indian eyes. Often an older boy, or a chief, who was known for his keen sight, judged the contest, but much of the time the players made the decision after each throw. The painted end helped the judging but it took sharp eyes to follow the whirling stick after three or four throws had been made. Modern players should *never* attempt to catch the turning stick.

Skill Games

About Web Weaving (Cat's Cradle)

Today, this string game is, unfortunately, too little known in the United States. It has been played by millions of children and grownups all over the world for many thousands of years and is still popular in many countries. The game is supposed to have originated in China but it was equally well known in Japan, the Philippines, and far-off Australia and New Guinea. Web weaving probably reached the American Indians and the Eskimo by way of the Orient hundreds of years before the white men settled in their territory. The grownups, both men and women, firmly believed there was magic in web weaving and that spirits sometimes came to criticize or admire the artistic and intricate designs formed under the swiftly weaving fingers. The youngsters did not take this string game quite so seriously but they did like to weave patterns of animals, tipi doors, and a more easily made design known both as "fish spear" and "chicken's foot," and would spend hours patiently working out new forms of the craft.

The Navaho say that their forefathers were taught to play web weaving by the Spider People, while the Zuni declare that the design is the netted shield of the War Gods and that the game was given to them by Grandmother Spider. The Algonquin were fond of web weaving as were the Teton Dakota, who called it the *Game of String wrapped in and out among the fingers.* Most tribes made string figures that bore some resemblance to animals, birds, stars, hills, and lakes or any other interesting and more intricate designs that occurred to them. Most experts among the American Indians worked out their figures alone, using teeth and toes, and lips and weights to hold the string in place when needed, without a partner to help them manipulate or hold the strings. In their efforts to do with only two hands a job that in many cases could have been much easier to do with four, it is easy to understand why teeth and stones were used to hold the string down and in place, while their fingers prepared to take a new hold on the web. The Indians considered the steps in making the figures as only a means to an end—the finished design.

Today, cat's cradle is considered a "girl's game" by some boys, who leave the playing of it to their sisters. This is a mistake, for all boys should be handy with string and knotting and cat's cradle helps to develop this skill. While modern players sometimes decide on the most suitable length of string for the size of their hands by using a piece of string which can be wound eight times around their knuckles, experts at web weaving, who play the game with the same zeal as some chess players devote to chess, use different lengths of string for various sets of figures. For beginners and average players, strong, medium-weight twine in about 68-inch lengths is suitable for most designs and provides a little leeway in handling various patterns. The two ends of the cord may be joined exactly with a square knot, also known as a reef knot, but real experts would not dream of *tying* the two ends together—they splice or weave them together!

Players of this string game who find it difficult to work individually, in the Indian way, will find it much easier to "weave webs" with a partner. One of the easiest Indian patterns, made by one weaver, follows. Easier designs, for partners working together, follow the Fish Spear.

FISH SPEAR

An individual weaver holds the string in a different manner and follows a different opening than when partners work on the same patterns.

In the position A, the string is held on the thumb and little finger of each hand with the string across the palm of the hand, as shown in the diagram.

In B, insert the right index finger from *above* behind the string at the left palm. Draw the loop out to the right, twisting it three or four times by revolving the index finger.

In C, with the left index finger, pick up the string at the right palm from *below*. It must be picked up *through* the loop at the right index finger, between the twist and the finger. Separate the hands and draw the strings tight. Release the loops from the right thumb and right little finger and separate the hands.

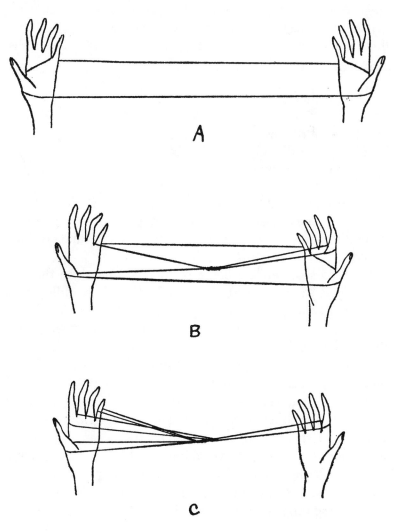

A

B

C

PATTERNS FOR PARTNERS

The real fun in web weaving is experimenting. Sometimes interesting and pretty patterns appear when least expected. The string patterns which follow are the less difficult ones mentioned, as they are formed by two partners working together. The diagrams illustrate this form of the game. The three fingers which do the work are indicated as follows in the drawings:

1—the thumb
2—index finger
5—the little finger
(3—the middle finger, used only
in the opening position)

In opening A, put both hands up through the circle of string, making a single loop around each hand. The string passes around the index finger, across the back of each hand, as illustrated.

Now, pass the middle finger of the right hand up through the loop at the palm of the left hand. With the middle finger of the left hand, pick up the loop at the palm of the right hand, in the same way. You now have the opening or starting position, shown in Figure B.

Your partner joins the game at this point and puts thumb and index finger of each hand down through the crossed strings on each side, as indicated by numbers 1 and 2 in Figure B. The thumb and index finger are brought together at the tips so that the string cannot escape. Then, they come across the two outside strings, around and underneath, coming up through the center. The hands are now pulled apart to make the string taut, and the thumb and forefinger opened out, making the pattern shown in Figure C.

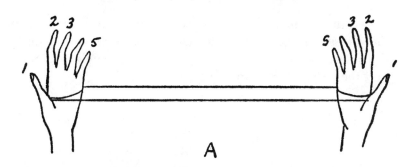

A

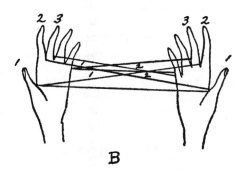

B

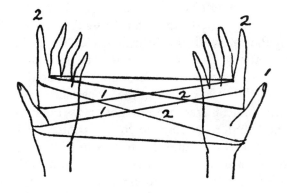

C

193

Pass the thumb and index finger of each hand down through the crossed strings and bring them across, around and under the outside strings, bringing the hands up through the center. Pull the strings taut, and you have Figure D.

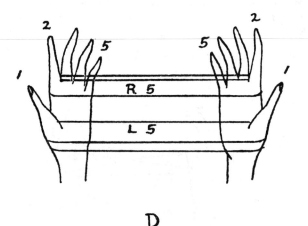

D

Your partner now takes the center string on the right side with the little finger of the left hand, pulls it a little to the left, then reaches through the arch thus formed and takes the center string on the left with the little finger of the right hand and pulls it a little to the right. In this way, the strings are now crossed. Your partner must be careful to hold each string tightly with the little fingers so that it cannot escape. Now the thumbs and index fingers are brought across the outside strings, around and under, coming up in the center, as before. The strings are pulled taut, and this results in Figure E.

The strings are already crossed, so all you have to do is pass the thumb and index finger through the crossed strings on each side and bring the hands out, around, over and *down* through the outer strings. This movement is the opposite of the usual way in which the hands are brought *up* through the outer strings. Now you have what appears to be Figure C again.

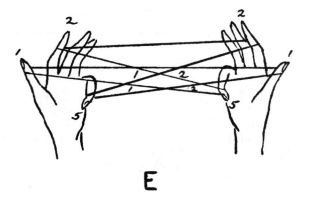

E

Actually it is a little different, because it, in turn, leads to Figure F which is quite different from the others.

Your partner puts thumb and index finger down through the crossed strings, as in Figure C, brings them across, around and under the outer strings, bringing the hands up in the center. The strings are pulled taut and you have Figure F.

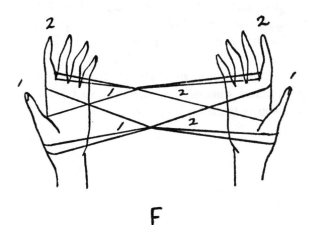

F

You now put the thumb and index finger down through the crossed strings and bring the hands up through the center. When the strings are pulled taut, Figure G makes its appearance.

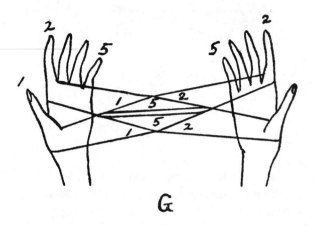

G

Here again, there are two loose strings in the center which must be crossed. As in Figure D, your partner picks up these two center strings, one with each little finger, and crosses them as before, also passing thumb and index finger of each hand down through the crossed strings at each side, bringing the hands up in the center. When the string is pulled tight, the result is a combination of Figures E and G.

Dozens of patterns can be achieved as the game continues— many pretty and unexpected. Strings must be kept taut to assure an even pattern on both sides.

9.

Guessing Games

THESE GAMES have usually been called games of chance or hazard, but the term "guessing game" covers all of them equally well. Some expert players of a considerable number of these games would have been offended by any one of these terms. They believed that they were gifted with extrasensory perception, or that their knowledge of psychology aided them in their search for the hand which held the stick or counter. Other good players were certain that the charms painted on their sticks helped the thrown sticks to fall or jump as the owner wished. Some players, through incessant practice and considerable concentration, developed the art of bouncing guessing sticks on a rock or other surface so that they could tell in advance exactly how the sticks would fall, thus assuring the desired score. Despite the beliefs and the skill involved in playing some of the games, a few representative games— selected from a great many—have been listed in this chapter as Guessing Games. Most modern players will agree with this caption, after playing a few of them.

GUESSING STICKS

These measured from a little over 1 inch in length to 15 inches or more, and ranged from wheat-straw thickness to about 1¼ inches. When they were arranged under a mat or blanket, prior to guesses being made as to which stick was marked in a certain way, the longer sticks were used, though long sticks were also used when the sticks were sorted rapidly in the open, in plain view, and then held out or stacked in bundles. These "sticks" were often made from branches, twigs, reeds, rushes, and straws. They represented arrow shafts, old Indians say. Many of the sticks were artistically decorated, in a way which did not help the guessers to be able to locate the odd stick they were usually looking for. That is why most of these guessing sticks were marked with a painted band at one end, both ends, or in the middle of the stick. In this way the distinguishing marks painted on them could easily be hidden by the hands or fingers.

The disks used in guessing games were hidden in different ways. On the Northwest Pacific Coast the disks were nearly always hidden in shredded cedar bark, while in other parts of the United States they were hidden under a blanket or mat.

COUNTING OR TALLY STICKS

These were used as counters in guessing games. Varying in length from 6 to 15 inches, they measured anywhere from ½ to ¾ inches in diameter. Many were pointed at one end so that they could easily be stuck into the ground while keeping score. Most of them were decorated with burned or painted stripes and other markings, while others were simply painted red or yellow, without other decoration.

SINGING DURING GUESSING GAMES

Many tribes throughout the United States sang in a body or had special groups of singers sing throughout the entire length of the Guessing Games, which frequently lasted all night or longer. Sometimes the players who were hiding the disk or reed sang while hiding these counters, and at other times those who were about to do the guessing sang. The songs and singing varied greatly among the different tribes and for the many different guessing games. At times the singing was monotonous, while at others the songs were of a wild nature, covering the entire Indian scale of music. Sometimes, especially on the Northwest Coast, the author has heard singing during guessing contests which could only be described as eerie and unearthly. How even the most stoic Indian could possibly concentrate while playing and listening to such "music" was a thought that came after wondering how any human beings, apart from shamans, could possibly produce such weird sounds!

While a number of guessing games were in progress, such as the Eleven Stick Game, favored by the Cree, there was neither singing nor singers.

CEREMONIAL GUESSING GAMES

A considerable number of guessing games were full-dress affairs and involved much ceremony—prior to the start, sometimes during the game, and when the games came to an end, perhaps fifteen hours after their commencement. Because of the ceremonial character of a certain number of these games, the writer has placed a few of them in the chapter on "Ceremonial Games" in order that the Indian methods of play may be illustrated.

ELEVEN STICK GAME

Plains

BOYS	2 TO 6 PLAYERS	INDOORS
ELEMENTARY—SENIOR	INDIVIDUAL—TEAM	OR OUTDOORS

This game is generally played by two seated players. The only equipment needed is eleven thin sticks, 18 inches long and about 1/16 of an inch in diameter. One player rapidly divides the sticks into two bundles so that one bundle has six sticks and the other only five. The arrangement of the sticks is either done under a blanket or in the open, because the shuffling of the sticks is carried out with such surprising speed that it is impossible for the eye to follow the movements made by the flying fingers. The guesser indicates which bundle has the six sticks by touching the back of the hand which he thinks holds them. The guessing is done with almost equal rapidity, so that many games are played in an amazingly short time. Tally sticks are used to keep track of the score and the players take turns at guessing.

FOUR STICK GAME

Northwest Coast—Southwest

| BOYS OR GIRLS | 2 TO 6 PLAYERS | INDOORS |
| JUNIOR—SENIOR | INDIVIDUAL | OR OUTDOORS |

This is one of the most interesting forms of the almost countless guessing games played by Indians throughout the Americas. The Chinook artistically decorated the four hardwood sticks they used in the game. The four sticks used were all 12 inches long, but two of them were only about ½ inch in diameter and they were tightly wrapped from end to end with a narrow strip of buckskin. The other two sticks were 1 inch thick in the middle and tapered down to about ½ inch in diameter at both ends. These two sticks were ornamented with a burned or painted stripe design. The Indian Cliff Dwellers of Arizona played this game with four sticks 7 inches long. The game was played in this way.

One player challenged another and both players sat on the ground facing each other. One of them arranged the sticks under a round mat about 18 inches in diameter, in any of the six ways shown in the drawing. Players took turns guessing the arrangement. Often a player who guessed correctly continued to guess until he guessed wrongly, when the other player did the guessing. Sticks 8 inches long, sharpened at one end, then painted red, were used as tally sticks. They were stuck in the ground in front of the players to record the correct guesses made by each in the course of the game.

●●●●   ●●●●   ●●●●   ●●●●   ●●●●   ●●●●

WHAT DO I HOLD?

Northwest Coast

GIRLS	2 TO 20 PLAYERS	OUTDOORS
ELEMENTARY—JUNIOR	INDIVIDUAL	OR INDOORS

This was a favorite game with Indian girls of all ages. It is played with all sorts of small, natural objects such as a tree leaf, blade of grass, one of several berries, pieces of bone, pebbles of various colors, shells, pieces of colored cloth, earrings, and other objects small enough to conceal in the hand. One girl holds an object in one closed hand while the other girl or girls guess what the object is.

When the guessers have difficulty in guessing they may ask, "Is it round?" or "Is it red?" or "Is it smooth?" and similar questions which require only to be answered by "Yes" or "No." The girl who first guesses correctly takes the place of the one who has hidden the object. Gifted with considerable patience and not being bothered with many distractions, the Indian girls often played this simple game for hours on end. They preferred it because it offered more variety than such other guessing games as those in which the player or players only had to guess which hand held a pebble, for instance.

Modern players, playing indoors, have perhaps a far greater choice of small objects that may easily be concealed in one hand than did the Indian girls who usually played this game outdoors, using objects donated by Mother Nature.

ONE PEBBLE GAME
Northwest Coast

| BOYS OR GIRLS | 2 TO 6 PLAYERS | OUTDOORS |
| ELEMENTARY—JUNIOR | INDIVIDUAL | OR INDOORS |

Often when an elderly Chinook went out to meet a friend from another tribe, he was absent from his village for many hours or failed to return at all until someone was sent to bring him back. The reason was simple. The two men were so busily engaged in playing the One Pebble Game that time had been forgotten.

This game was played by two men sitting facing each other. Each had a small round pebble, about ¾ inch in diameter, and took turns at passing it from hand to hand in front of them and concealing it in one hand, while humming a monotonous tune to disconcert and throw the other player off balance. The guesser pointed to the hand which he believed contained the pebble. That hand was instantly opened and if the guesser was wrong, the other player had another turn. When the guesser was correct, he took over. The game was played at unbelievable speed, a dozen or more games being played in a few minutes. Though this game is played all over the globe, in various forms, it is also an authentic Indian game.

GUESS STICK

Plains—Northwest Coast—Woodland—Southwest

BOYS OR GIRLS	2 TO 6 PLAYERS	INDOORS
ELEMENTARY—SENIOR	INDIVIDUAL	OR OUTDOORS

This is the adult Indian Two Stick Guessing Game, one of the many so-called "Hand Games," which was played by countless Indians throughout the Americas. They generally used two sticks each 1½ inches long and about ¼ inch thick. One of the sticks had either a short length of thread tied around the center or a little burned or painted line, to indicate that it was *the* stick. Indian children often imitated their parents by playing this simple guessing game.

The two players sat facing each other a little distance apart and the one who had the first chance to manipulate the sticks did so behind his back. He then brought his hands around in front of him, palms down, and the guesser pointed to or touched the back of the hand which he believed held *the* stick. If he was wrong, he kept on trying until he guessed correctly. Then the guesser got his turn to handle the sticks.

The players of some tribes kept up a low, monotonous humming while handling the sticks in order to throw their guessing opponents off balance, while others made a series of lightning-fast rhythmic motions with their hands and arms as a part of stick concealment, which was almost enough to mesmerize the

average guesser. Many stick manipulators made the changes
from hand to hand while facing their opponents, with the
stick-holding hands in front of them, but the changes were
made with such lightning speed and in such an entirely deceptive manner that no doubt the guesser would have preferred
that the stick shifts be made in the more orthodox, behind-the-
back manner. Guess Stick would not be a particularly intel-
lectual game were it not for the psychological tricks which can
be employed in order to deceive an opponent. A stick holder
will sometimes extend his hands, backs up, advancing one hand
rather obviously. His naïve smile suggests that he wishes to
make things easier, much easier, for his opponent. The guesser
is too wary to accept such dubious help and, naturally, points
to or touches the back of the hand that is held rather shyly in
the background. Yes, *the* stick was in the more outstretched
hand!

HIDDEN BALL*

Plains—Woodland—Northwest Coast—Southwest

BOYS OR GIRLS   4 TO 10 PLAYERS   INDOORS
ELEMENTARY—JUNIOR   INDIVIDUAL   OR OUTDOORS

The Indian game of *find the hidden ball* was played in one
form or another practically throughout the Americas. A number of tribes hid the small pebble or ball in one of several
specially made containers, while others hid it in other ways.
This game is classed with the Moccasin Game, where a bullet
or bead was hidden in a moccasin. A game just as difficult for
both the guessers and the player hiding the ball can be played
in this way.

A blanket or mat is spread on the floor or ground, after it
has been folded in half. Then the chief or player who hides the
small ball conceals it so that the other players, who sit in a
fairly large circle around the blanket, cannot tell under which

corner of the folded blanket the ball has been placed. One small, red sponge rubber ball, 1 inch in diameter or less, will serve as the ball; or a marble, still more difficult to detect, may be used. The player who hides the ball can use all of the Indian methods of distracting the guessers' attention while hiding the ball. He can appear to hide it, with elaborate pantomime and strange sounds and gestures, under the first corner of the blanket or mat he comes to. Then he carries on and appears to hide it, with less fuss, under another corner. The guessers, who are quite certain, by his antics, that he has *not* hidden the ball where he pretended to, are astonished to see, after the guess has been made, that he did exactly that.

The game is best played when one guesser is chosen for all of the players, and announces where the majority of them believe the ball to be hidden. This confines the guessing to one guess, which makes for good play. Another way is to let each player guess in turn. The player who guesses correctly hides the next ball or marble.

KNOTTY

Southwest

BOYS OR GIRLS	2 TO 18 PLAYERS	OUTDOORS
ELEMENTARY—SENIOR	INDIVIDUAL—TEAM	OR INDOORS

For this guessing game, all that is required is a length of stout cord or a piece of thin rope 18 inches long for each of two individual players or a team. This is how the game is played.

Two players sit face to face with about 8 feet between them. One player holds his length of cord in front of him and the other player is the guesser. When the player who is guessing says "Ready!" the other player puts his cord behind him and makes any number of simple, single knots on it, from none to four. When he has made the knots, which he should do as speedily as possible, he brings his empty hand in front of him and his opponent then guesses how many knots there are on the cord. He has only one guess.

Immediately the guess is made, the cord is held out in front of the player who made the knots, in order to prove the guesser right or wrong. A little psychological fun may be introduced into the game by copying the play-ways of the Indian player. He usually took most time to make no knot or only one. His face often gave the impression, while his fingers behind him were idle, that he was working hard to make at least the maximum number of knots—four. When it came to the showdown, however, the cord showed only one or two knots, if any. Some Pueblo players raced nimble fingers to tie four knots in the time usually taken to tie one knot, all of which made it hard for the guesser to keep up with the tricks used to deceive.

When two teams, of four to six players in each, contest, each player on each team has a turn at knotting and guessing before the winning side counts coup. A team may have a brief conference before guessing the number of knots made by the rival player. In team play, a referee is usually chosen to keep a tally of the score made by each team. He often uses pieces of twigs or grass, or other counters, to keep track, working in full view of each team as he records the score.

In modern play, as many as six knots can be made, but four knots assures a good game.

10.

Group Challenge-Games

BEAR CAVE CHIEF*
Northwest Coast

BOYS   2 TO 12 PLAYERS   OUTDOORS
JUNIOR—SENIOR   INDIVIDUAL—TEAM

This is an amusing rough-and-tumble game which delights
the spectators. It is best contested by two boys of about the
same height and weight. The only equipment needed is four
wooden hoops, each about 20 inches in diameter. These hoops
may be 2 or 3 inches less in diameter but not more than 2
inches larger. The chief in charge of this contest should make
absolutely certain that every hoop used is perfectly smooth.
If sandpaper does not accomplish this, each hoop can be carefully wrapped entirely around with a long strip or a number of
shorter pieces of adhesive tape, so that there are neither rough
places nor slivers exposed on the rim. Even metal hoops treated
in this way will serve, should wooden hoops of some sort not
be available.

This challenge is adapted from one contested by Indian boys
on the Canadian Northwest Coast, and represents a race between two or more "bears" to take possession of a cave. The
four hoops represent four caves. These hoops are held upright

in place by four strong chiefs, equal distances apart around a circle 40 feet in diameter. A marker, which can be a strip of cloth or a paper plate, is stapled halfway between any two markers, as the starting point. Two contestants, on hands and knees, face in the same direction, one on each side of the marker, waiting for the signal to start.

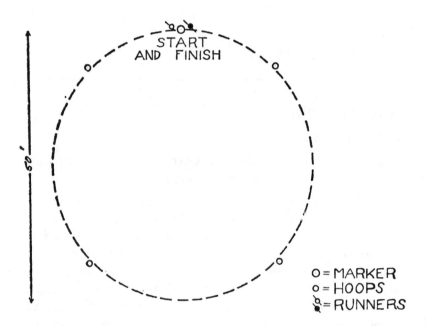

O = MARKER
o = HOOPS
🐻 = RUNNERS

When the chief in charge shouts "Search!" both bears crawl as fast as possible toward the first hoop. Should both bears reach the hoop at the same time, the fun begins. Each bear should try to shoulder the other one out of the way in order to crawl through the hoop first. Hands and feet must not be used at any time. Once a bear has his head inside a hoop, he is allowed to crawl through it without further interference from his opponent. The other bear follows after him as quickly as possible and tries to reach the second hoop ahead of his rival or at least at the same time. The contest continues through the other hoops until the contestant-bear who first crawls through the fourth, and last, hoop and reaches the starting marker counts coup and wins.

More fun and obstruction can be caused by having three or four bears instead of two "race" over the same course in the same manner. Each bear is on his own.

The most mirthful way to carry out this challenge is to have the two rival bears start out from the marker in opposite directions on the command "Search!" Not only speed but chance enters into this contest, for the point where the bears meet may decide which bear will be the first to count coup. If the bears pass each other between the cave entrances, there will be no clash at the cave mouths and speed may decide the race. On the other hand, if the bears meet head on at a hoop, one on each side of it, of course they may *push, not bump,* head on, to see which can force the right of way. The bear who first succeeds in getting his head through the hoop wins right of way and his rival must withdraw and let him crawl through first. The same rule applies when a bear manages to push his head through a hoop just before his rival arrives. The chiefs who hold the hoops should see that neither bear uses hands or feet in the scuffles at any point, nor can hands be used to help a bear through a hoop.

When three or four bears are on each of two teams, they contest this race in relay fashion. The teams line up at the starting point, facing in the direction or directions decided by the chief, and the second bear on each team starts out to make a round of the caves just as soon as his bear-mate returns to the starting marker. In this way each bear on the team touches off his bear-mate until every bear has gone through all four hoops and returned to the starting point. The first team to finish, after all of its members have circled the circle correctly, counts coup and wins.

Of course, to add Northwest Coast Indian realism to this contest, it must be remembered that bears in search of suitable caves are often not too even-tempered and there is no rule which keeps one bear from going after the other, but always on all fours, and shouldering him around a bit, in order to slow him down when they meet at any point between hoops. Fortunately, bears on the lookout for a cave have to hurry, as a rule, and have not too much time for scuffling. The chief in charge of the contest should point this out before the contest gets underway.

THERE AND BACK*

Northwest Coast

BOYS	4 TO 10 PLAYERS	OUTDOORS
JUNIOR—SENIOR	PARTNERS	OR INDOORS

This is the adaptation of a game which the author watched Indian boys play on the Canadian Northwest Coast. The game, as described, can be played equally well by modern Indians and is certain to cause amusement to the spectators. Two lines are marked on the ground, one exactly opposite the other, 40 feet apart. One player kneels facing one of these lines on hands and knees, with finger tips resting on the line. His racing partner goes down on hands and knees, a little way behind, facing in the opposite direction. A chief ties one ankle of the two players together with a strong strip of cloth. Each team of two partners in the race is fastened together in this way, with a distance of 4 feet between teams.

When the chief shouts "Go!" each team "races" away from the starting line, the boy with finger tips on it advancing head first toward the second line while his unfortunate partner has to race backward. Each pair of partners tries to co-ordinate their movements in order to advance as swiftly as possible. This is easy to write about but hard to actually accomplish!

When the racer advancing toward the line, head first, is able to touch it with his finger tips, he shouts "Back!" whereupon his partner, who now has the pleasure of facing forward as he crawls, sets off at top speed back to the starting line, his partner following as best he can. The first team to return to the starting line, with both partners crawling on their knees, wins, just as soon as the leading partner touches the line with his finger tips.

As will be seen from the text, the chief tied one ankle of each pair of players together. A second version is for both players to race with *both* ankles tied to those of his partner. Both ways are good fun for all concerned but progressing in one version will be found considerably more difficult than in the other!

STOP!

Plains—Northwest Coast

BOYS AND GIRLS	6 TO 18 PLAYERS	OUTDOORS
ELEMENTARY—SENIOR	INDIVIDUAL	OR INDOORS

This is a dance step game which many Plains Indians and other tribes enjoyed in various forms. The only equipment required is either a drum, tom-tom, or, as frequently used on the Northwest Coast, a hardwood plank about 2 feet square and any thickness from ½ to 1 inch, to serve as a drum. Two improvised drumsticks complete the gear and they should be used by a drummer with a good sense of rhythm and timing. The drummer can sit behind a blanket, out of sight of the dancers, though a really good drummer can sit in the open, even in the middle of a circle of dancers, and still count coup. This is how some tribes, such as the Lakotah, played the game.

The drummer commences to beat the drum and the dancers move around in a circle trying to keep time to the music, but they must stop stepping instantly when the drum beat stops. This may leave some alert dancers with one foot in the air, and it must be kept there until the drum commences again. The drummer tries to trick the dancers into stopping at the wrong moment, by slowing up the beat suddenly, then starting out on fast time, to stop a second later. A chief can referee the game and see that those who stop dancing at the wrong moment leave the dance circle.

After each stop, either the chief or the drummer says "Dance!" and the dancers resume the dance. The drummer, of course, must drum without unintentional pauses, though he may change the tempo as often as he likes, because the slightest pause may lead some dancers to believe that it is the stop signal when the drummer does not intend it to be. Dancers who stop at the wrong times through the fault of the drummer are not ruled out of the game.

While the Indians danced rhythmically and kept good time to the drum music, younger modern players who have little knowledge of dance steps or tempo can still have fun jumping from foot to foot, or on both feet, as they move around the circle.

LANCE HOLD

Plains—Northwest Coast

BOYS   12 TO 18 PLAYERS   OUTDOORS
JUNIOR—SENIOR   TEAM   OR INDOORS

For this challenge-game a "lance" is made from a straight hardwood pole. It can be from 6 to 8 feet in length and about 1 inch in diameter, rounded at each end. This lance can be painted in some bright, light color, yellow or orange, for example. Two lines, each ½ inch wide, are painted in red or black around the lance so that each line is 4½ inches from the exact center. Two other lines are marked in the same way, 10 inches from each end of the lance. These distances are suggested for two teams of six players in each. Longer lances can be used and stripes marked farther from the ends and center when the contesting teams are larger. This is worked out proportionately in order to give the increased number of players a chance to have a hand in the game. Instead of paint stripes, strips of colored adhesive tape can be used for markings on the lance, which allows the distances to be increased or decreased by changing strips when distances are changed.

For modern Indians, the game can be carried out in this way. Two teams, of six to nine players, face each other in two straight lines 30 feet apart. A chief stands exactly halfway between the two lines, in line with the last players on either end. He holds the lance upright with one hand on one end of the lance and the other end rests on the ground. The top of the lance is held so that it can be released instantly. The chief tells the contestants that when he lets the lance fall to the ground between the two lines, immediately it touches the ground, but not a second before, they may rush forward. From either side, they are to try to grasp the lance, with the *left* hand only, anywhere between its two ends, *but* the center section of the lance, between the two stripes, counts grand coup and equals two hands in the scoring. The section marked off at each end counts coup and equals one and a half hands when scoring at the end of the contest. A left hand on all other parts of the lance counts one hand. The lance must not be carried more than 10 feet away from where it fell when dropped by the chief and it must not be raised more than shoulder high at any time during the contest. Actually the lance is best held at about waist level throughout the struggle. Right hands must not be used for any purpose at any time, and the players should be cautioned before the rush begins that they must not try to shoulder each other out of position. The challengers who fail to grasp the lance in any one of the three places which count coup may still use their left hands in order to try to get a handhold somewhere else on the lance. The chief in charge of the challenge, as soon as the rush begins, starts counting, fairly slowly, up to 60 and then shouts "Hold!" All players must "freeze" instantly on this command and those who grab or move their hands after it has been given are disqualified. The chief counts the left hands on the lance, and the team wins which has the highest score made by left hands squarely on the lance. A hand on top of another hand or partially on top of another hand does not score.

Another version of this challenge-game is to count *only* the left hands on the grand coup and coup sections of the lance—center and ends only. Other variations will suggest themselves to modern chiefs, such as allowing the challengers to grasp the lance with both hands, placed separately only, or together only, or barring the hold of the lance in the middle grand coup section.

Big, rival groups of Indians used to contest this challenge on a 10 or 12 foot lance, with no sections marked—and no holds barred!

SIT POLE PULL

Northwest Coast

BOYS   6 TO 12 PLAYERS   OUTDOORS

JUNIOR—SENIOR   INDIVIDUAL—TEAM   OR INDOORS

This game was played by men and boys of some of the Northwest Coast tribes, who may have learned it from Eskimo neighbors, though a similar game has been played by some Woodland tribes. As usual when a game is played in far-spread sections of the country, there are slight variations in the form of play. However, plenty of amusement and challenge will be found in contesting it in any one of the following ways. A stout, smooth pole 8 to 10 feet long and about 1 or 1½ inches in diameter is the only gear required. The length is based on the number of contestants taking part. The pole is laid on the ground and from three to six players sit along either side of it at opposite ends, and as close to their end as possible. The players sit partly inside each other's legs, with the legs spread out for balance. The pole is held only with the right hand and when in pulling position it is held about waist level.

On the word "Pull!" each team tries to pull the other toward it, without themselves giving ground. The game should be played on smooth ground when played outdoors, so that there is nothing to brace the feet against. Various versions of this challenge can be carried out. The pulling may be done with only the left hands, or both hands, for example.

Two players, one on each end of the pole, can contest this game as an individual challenge.

BIG HURRY POLE*

Northwest Coast

BOYS   12 TO 24 PLAYERS   OUTDOORS
SENIOR   TEAM

Another suitable name for this rough-and-tumble contest besides the translation of the Chinook jargon name for this game, *Hyas Hyak Stick,* could be Pole Raiders. In its original form it was a hard-fought, near-battle contest disputed by fifteen to forty warriors from each of two tribes or clans. This is how it was carried out on the Northwest Coast.

One clan set up a heavy pole, about 3 feet above floor level, just inside a big house. The challengers of that clan stood behind this barrier and tried to prevent an equal number, more or less, of warriors from a rival clan from getting either over or under the pole and so into the house. Quarter was neither given nor asked in such free-for-all encounters, especially when rivalry was intense—as it usually was. About the only rules that were supposed to be observed were the few which did not permit either defenders or attackers to use knives, clubs, or other lethal weapons on each other during the encounter. When the author spoke with an old House Chief, who used to be one of the referees at such raids, the chief was careful to explain that the judges never allowed the challenge to become *really* rough. Just as soon as an overenthusiastic player flashed a knife or produced and swung a hitherto concealed war club, a House Chief promptly hit that player on the skull with a club. "No trouble he gave—after!" explained the old chief, his eyes aglow with memories of how he had helped to keep such hard-fought challenges free from rough stuff.

Should a present-day chief of modern Indians decide to skip this hearty challenge, without reading further, there are many considerably tamer ones set down in this book. If the decision is to go ahead, here is how this highly competitive challenge can be carried out in a safe and more friendly fashion under the strict supervision of several chiefs. A strong smooth pole, about 16 feet long and 18 inches in diameter, is securely fastened, horizontally, with the lower side 28 inches above the ground, in the middle of an entirely smooth, stone-free piece of ground. This pole may either be very securely lashed at each end to two stout, smooth, round poles 10 inches in diameter and about 6 feet 10 inches long or set up in another way, described later. The end of each pole mentioned should be inserted for a length of 3 feet into a tight-fitting hole, made in advance with a post hole digger. The cross pole is steadier when these two supporting poles have to be driven into the prepared holes. Another good way to support the horizontal pole is illustrated in the diagram. In this method of support, at each end of the horizontal pole there are two poles 6 feet 10 inches long and 6 inches in diameter, one on each side. The long pole is best lashed to the supporting poles with fairly thin, strong rope tied with a clove hitch and well-tightened by further lashing and frapping. A notch may be cut near the top of each upright pole, if necessary, to assure that the lashings

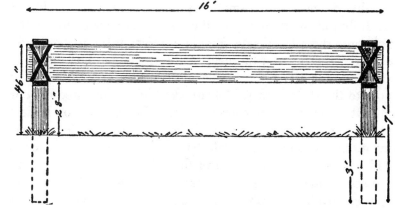

remain in place without slipping, holding the horizontal pole 46 inches above ground at all points of its length when the waves and weight of assault hit it during the challenge. Good clothes should *not* be worn for this contest! It is best played in either bare or stockinged feet, unless the chief allows sneakers to be worn.

The chief in charge of the melee has from six to twelve challengers from each team line up on each side of the Big Hurry Pole and 10 feet distant from it. He also posts two assistants, or one at least, on each side of the pole to see that rough stuff is reduced to a minimum and to help referee the raid. These deputy chiefs should *not* be armed with clubs. The chief in charge then picks one team to be the raiders. He warns them *not* to attempt to jump over the pole in any circumstances, nor stand on it, but tells them that they may try to climb over it or crawl under it. The defenders are then told to advance to their side of the pole, ready to repel the invaders, and the chief shouts "Attack!" Now the air rings with the war whoops, shouts, gasps, and cries of straining warriors locked in deadly combat.

There are a few simple but important rules for the judges to enforce. All of the attackers who succeed in crossing over or under the pole, clear of the defenders, count coup and should go over to a designated spot. The attackers should not willfully pull or drag any of the defenders over or under the pole onto the raiders' side. Should a defender be dragged over or under the pole, in the heat of the tussle, he must not take any further part in the scuffle until he has gone around the pole to the defenders' side again. At the end of three or four minutes, the chief in charge checks the number of raiders remaining. If more than half of them have succeeded in surmounting the Big Hurry Pole barrier, the raiders count coup and win. Should exactly half of the raiders have succeeded in the assault and reached the other side of the barrier, the contest is considered a tie. Should more than half of the raiders still remain on the wrong side of the pole, the defenders are the coup counters and winners. Should enough votes decide for a return match, after both sides have regained breath, the raiders become the defenders for the second match.

Modern chiefs should experiment with various rules and methods for contesting this challenge-game. For instance, a defender pulled over or under the pole onto the raiders' side, with or without intent on the part of the raiders, can be instantly ruled out of the contest and sent to a spot, decided on before the raid, where he will be removed from temptation's call to rejoin the fray. The drawback to this form of the challenge lies in the fact that after a few minutes it is hard to tell by their actions whether a contestant is a raider or defender, or which team is which! Having each team wear identifying armbands may save a lot of alert refereeing on the part of the chiefs. If the version just given is carried out, it is probably best for the chief in charge not to designate one side as raiders and the other as defenders but let each team try to pull its rivals across to their side. Immediately a member of either team is pulled to the opposite side, he is out of the game and leaves the pole contest area. In this version the chief can halt the fray after a few minutes and announce the winning side, after having counted the number of contestants still in action in each team. The contest always requires alert and able judging and handling to assure each side a square deal and make certain that nobody is injured in the tussle.

Hyas Hyak Stick, as carried out on the Northwest Coast, was a free-for-all with the most nebulous rules. Nobody retired from the fray, unless clubbed by a referee, while he was able to stand or crawl and the contest continued until complete exhaustion called a halt. Despite this the winners were heartily acclaimed and feted.

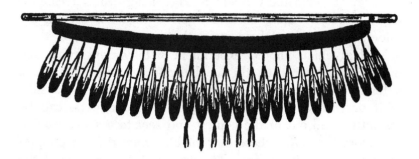

CIRCLE BREAK
Northwest Coast—Woodland

BOYS	4 TO 8 PLAYERS	OUTDOORS
JUNIOR—SENIOR	INDIVIDUAL	OR INDOORS

This is another of the numerous push-pull challenge-games played by many tribes scattered throughout the Americas. These games provided fun, gave a good chance to those who wanted to try or exhibit their strength, and had the great advantage of requiring no equipment. Thus the challenge could be contested on the spur of the moment, at any place, and with only two players or more. This game has been selected by the author as the safest of the finger and hand pulling games, where hardy Indians thought little of disjointed fingers suffered in many of such contests. In this challenge, when a contestant feels he has had enough he can release his grip before any real strain occurs.

Two sturdy players of about the same size and weight face each other. Each player forms a circle with his arms and hands by grasping his fingers in a lock-grip, as though he were closing his fists to box but instead of closing each hand separately he locks the fingers of one hand inside the other. This grip can be broken by either contestant by simply straightening out the fingers, and it will be seen that they are going to get plenty of help in so doing! The circle made by each player is interlocked by one player placing an arm through the circle made by the player facing him before locking his own hands together. The challengers now back away from each other until the circle, through strain, becomes more oval than round. At this point, two players of about the same weight join the game. Each one latches around the waist of either of the locked-together pair and begins to pull steadily in an effort to pull them apart, by a steady pull. The two players with interlocked arms endeavor not to be separated. After a moment or two, when the interlocked circles remain unbroken, two other players hitch onto the waists of the other two pulling players, one to each player, and this continues until the circle is broken and the two original players are pulled apart. The first of these two players either to break his handhold voluntarily or have it pulled open loses and his opponent counts coup.

BUFFALO HIDE*

Plains

BOYS OR GIRLS	4 TO 12 PLAYERS	OUTDOORS
ELEMENTARY—JUNIOR	INDIVIDUAL	OR INDOORS

Some of the Plains tribes played this strenuous game by taking a big buffalo hide and lacing a strong, woven rawhide thong around its four sides to form hand grips for the men and women players who stood all around it and held it at about waist level. They pulled it taut by leaning slightly backward and pulling on the handgrip thong.

Two fairly evenly matched players then got onto the center of the skin and tried to push each other off the tightly stretched skin. At times, and in some tribes, the contestants were a young warrior and a maiden. Quite often she was as strong

223

and active as the warrior—and she had to be to count coup as both shoved and pulled with all their might in order to force the other from the hide. The one remaining counted coup. Usually the contest was a fairly even one and quite often the maiden was the winner. The Indians were really tough and knew how to fall without hurting themselves, so this game was quite all right for them. Not only was the game somewhat hazardous for the actual contestants, but those who held the buffalo skin in place quite often were kicked in the face by moccasined feet or found themselves beneath two struggling contestants. This makes that amusing game unsuitable for modern Indians, who must be sent home by the chief in one piece. In these circumstances an adaptation is called for. Here it is.

The strength and skill of modern Indians can be tested equally well without the danger of a fall which might cause injury. This is done by spreading a big circle of canvas or strong cloth, about 9 feet in diameter, on the ground and having the contestants try to push each other off the circle. The best out of three bouts, if both players last that long, will decide the player who has the right to count coup. When a circle of cloth is not available, the game can be played on a large, old blanket, using a square instead of a circle for the contest. A circle marked on smooth soft ground will also serve the purpose. It is suggested that boy meet boy and girl meet girl in this rough-and-tumble game.

BUFFALO ROBE*

Plains

BOYS OR GIRLS   8 TO 20 PLAYERS   OUTDOORS
ELEMENTARY—JUNIOR INDIVIDUAL—TEAM

For this vigorous game, the Indians used to join hands in a big circle around a buffalo robe and when a chief shouted

"Pull!" they pulled and tugged in an effort to pull each other onto the skin. A player who touched it with his foot, or any other part of his body, dropped out of the game immediately. Modern Indians can play this amusing game in exactly the same way as the Blackfoot played it. Use a 5-foot square of strong cotton or other cloth to take the place of the buffalo robe. If it is dyed a dark brown it will not soil so soon. When this "robe" is spread out on the ground, the players form a circle around it, either holding hands or grasping each other's wrists. The latter way is probably better and it shows at once which player has released his hold. When the chief says "Ready!" the players all pull outward slightly, so that the circle is stretched tight. On the word "Pull!" all of the players pull and tug in an effort to pull their neighbors onto the robe without touching it themselves. Players may jump over the corners of the robe when in a position to do so. Any player who releases either of his hands more than once is disqualified. He then drops out of the circle and the remaining players close in a little. From time to time the chief should re-form the circle. When the entire circle of contestants manages to get beyond the robe, so that it is no longer within the circle, he must return the players and circle to the original position. As the number of contestants becomes less, the chief should also fold in the corners of the robe from time to time, to make it a little smaller.

Another version of this challenge, which makes it a team event, is to divide an even number of players, at least sixteen, into two or four teams and group each team in one half or one quarter of the circle. Of course the teams will automatically move around the circle in the course of the struggle. The team having the greatest number of players still in the circle after three or four minutes of play is the winner.

GRIZZLY GUARD*

Northwest Coast

BOYS OR GIRLS   6 TO 24 PLAYERS   OUTDOORS
ELEMENTARY—JUNIOR   INDIVIDUAL   OR INDOORS

A 30-foot circle is marked on the ground and from four to twenty players stand just outside it. In the middle of the circle, three sticks about 12 inches long and 1 inch in diameter are placed in a row, 1 foot apart. Rolled up sheets of strong brown paper replace the sticks quite well. Ten feet away from these sticks a player stands on a marker, or just beside one, so that he does not change his place. He holds one end of a strong cord or light rope 30 feet in length. The other end of the cord is attached to the belt of another player. He plays the part of the Grizzly Guard and crouches beside his Keeper, ready for instant action. His duty is to touch, if he can, all players who try to take one of the sticks. He can intercept them just as soon as they come within reach when they enter the circle, tag them as they make a dive for a stick, and can head them off and touch them as they leave the circle, with or without a stick.

The game begins when a chief gives the signal to start and continues until either all of the sticks have been taken by the raiders or all of those who try to secure the sticks have been put out of business by being touched by the grizzly. Any player touched while holding a stick must return it to its place in the center of the circle before leaving the circle, and the game.

The keeper of the grizzly cannot actually catch any of the attackers but he can use different ruses to help his bear. A little whispering between the grizzly and his keeper, during a lull in the attack, decides different ruses. For example, when the keeper suddenly points to one player within the circle and shouts "Get him!" the bear knows that he should touch another boy who appears to be within reach of a sudden dash by the bear but does not expect attack. When the keeper and bear appear to be off guard, as when the keeper scratches the bear's ear, is really the time when they are most on the alert and ready for instant action.

The rope which holds the bear can prove a handicap to raiders, who may trip over it or be blocked by it until tagged by the bear. The bear too can fall over the rope, to the joy of the raiders, even though a clumsy fall may be only a ruse to entice them within touching distance! Should the bear pull the rope from his keeper's hand, the attackers are awarded coup and a new game begins. Both bear and keeper should be changed fairly often, certainly with the start of each new game at least, so that other players may have the chance to play these exciting roles. A chief may make what rules he thinks best to avoid the sticks being rushed by all of the players at once, and similar contingencies. He may do so by letting only one side of a circle of players raid at the same time, or by having only two players from each side go after the sticks at the same time. The raiders should be told that it is not sporting merely to rush the sticks and grab for one, but that they should feint and circle and fool the bear while getting ready to snatch.

MEDICINE LODGE*·

Plains

BOYS	7 TO 12 PLAYERS	OUTDOORS
ELEMENTARY—JUNIOR	INDIVIDUAL	OR INDOORS

Indian boys played this game which in some respects resembles the old American game known as Stealing Sticks. Here is how it can most easily be played.

A square 12 feet in diameter is marked on the ground. This square is the Medicine Lodge. The challenger, playing the role of a medicine man, stands in the center of the lodge. He guards six sticks each about 10 inches long and 1¼ inches in diameter. They can be painted white. These sticks are laid separately in a circle around the medicine man, each one about 2 feet away from him. From four to six contestants surround the lodge. When a chief gives the "Attack" signal, each player tries to secure a stick without being touched on the hand by the medicine man. Only one stick at a time may be taken, and the contestant taking it is not safe until he has escaped without being touched on any part of the body by the defender of the sticks.

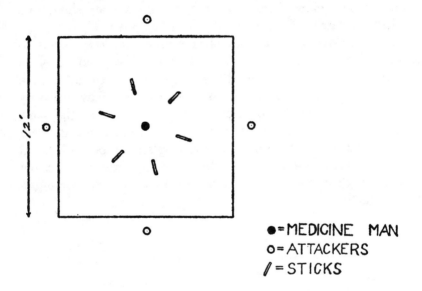

●=MEDICINE MAN
O=ATTACKERS
/ =STICKS

The chief directing the contest should instruct the attackers not to use the rush and grab method but to secure the sticks through a series of stealthy approaches and feints. These mislead the medicine man and are interesting and exciting for the spectators to watch. The contestant who gets the greatest number of sticks without being touched by the medicine man counts coup and wins.

An exciting addition may be made to this contest if the chief wishes. Should three players succeed in touching the medicine man *at the same moment*, before he can touch even one attacker, the medicine man becomes the prisoner of the attackers and they count coup and win. Throughout this challenge it requires an alert chief to decide who was touched by whom.

MEDICINE DRUM

Plains

BOYS	7 TO 12 PLAYERS	OUTDOORS
ELEMENTARY—JUNIOR	INDIVIDUAL	OR INDOORS

This challenge-game is carried out with the same size "lodge" marked in the same way as the one in the preceding challenge. Instead of using sticks, however, a small tom-tom or drum, which can easily be made as an arts and crafts project, takes their place. The medicine drum is placed in the center of the lodge with a drumstick laid on top of it. The medicine man is blindfolded, with the ears uncovered, and kneels directly beside the drum, on any side of it he wishes. Three contestants stand 3 paces away from and on different sides of the medicine lodge.

When the chief calls out "Attack!" the three attackers approach the drum as quietly as possible, try to pick up the stick and strike the drum, once, before the medicine man hears and touches the beater. A player touched is out of the contest and the remaining attackers take up their places again, outside of the lodge area. The chief in charge may have the attackers approach one at a time, signaling to the one whom he wishes to advance on the drum. Each player who gives the drum one stroke without being touched before the stick strikes the drum, counts coup. After each stroke on the drum the challenge recommences, the attackers starting again from their positions outside the lodge. Stealth, silence, and timing, not wild rushes, mark the skillful contestant in this challenge.

11.

Man-to-Man Challenge-Games

COUP STICK
Plains

BOYS	2 TO 6 PLAYERS	OUTDOORS
JUNIOR—SENIOR	INDIVIDUAL	OR INDOORS

A coup stick, of course, was a short "lance," usually blunt at both ends, which Indian warriors used for counting coups, such as touching armed enemies. An action of this sort counted more merits than actually striking an armed enemy with a lance or tomahawk, because of the risk involved by the unarmed coup. Such a stick was elaborately decorated with coup feathers and in other ways but, for the purpose of this challenge-game, all that is required is a stout hardwood pole, 4 feet long and 1 inch in diameter. It may be painted all over and decorated, only at each end, with a few feathers or colored cloth streamers, hanging down about 6 inches. Two challengers of about the same size and weight face each other and hold the coup stick, in the middle, with both hands at outstretched arm's length above and just in front of their heads. The right hands almost touch at the center of the stick and the left hand of each challenger is placed toward the middle of the stick, a little outside of the right hands.

231

When a chief shouts "Attack!" each contestant tries to take the stick away from his opponent by twisting his own arms and body in any way he likes, keeping his legs in the feet-astride position and trying to retain his hold on the stick while forcing his opponent to let go. A challenger may change his grip, when necessary, on the stick, but not more than an inch or two, and at least one hand must always grasp the coup stick. The challenger who first releases the stick with both hands is the loser. Such a challenge may be contested on the best-out-of-three-tries basis, but it is a strenuous contest and younger players should not be encouraged to contest three times running.

STRONG ARM

Plains—Woodland—Northwest Coast

BOYS   2 TO 6 PLAYERS   OUTDOORS
JUNIOR—SENIOR   INDIVIDUAL

The coup stick described in the preceding challenge may be used for this one, but the feathers or streamers at each end should be removed and those from one end suspended directly under the center of the stick. A line is drawn on the ground, or a long white feather is put on the ground to mark the central point of the challenge. Two sticks about 14 inches long and ½ inch in diameter are the only other gear needed for this challenge. This is how it is contested.

Two challengers of about the same size and weight each grasp an end of the coup stick with the right hand, holding the stick so that the feather or streamer attached to its center hangs directly over the mark on the ground. The chief now places one of the pieces of wood on the ground for each challenger, with an end one long pace away and the stick horizontal to and directly in line with the coup stick. When he calls "Attack!" each contestant pulls steadily on his end of the coup stick, trying to advance, sideways, so that he can reach and pick up

each skin and loudly challenges another brave to combat. When each skin has two contestants standing beside it—and the chief should see that they are fairly evenly matched—he places each pair 8 feet away from their pelt and lets them push, pull, and wrestle their way to it. The brave who first touches any part of the skunk skin with any part of his hand, arm, foot, leg, or body loses that bout. When the challenge is contested in this free-for-all manner, the chief must watch carefully to see that the match does not become too strenuously contested.

A less energetic form of contest is to have each pair of braves stand 8 feet away from the pelt with their hands grasping each other's shoulders, and push and pull until a foot touches any part of the pelt. Only the shoulder grip may be used in this version.

A still less strenuous form of this challenge, which nevertheless requires skill, strength, footwork, and agility, is decided by having each pair of contestants face each other, with one standing on either side of the skin. They grasp each other's shoulders and try to pull each other onto the skin. When they both, through pulling and straining, get some little distance away from it, they break away and recommence the struggle from the original position.

BACK!

Northwest Coast—Woodland

BOYS	2 TO 8 PLAYERS	OUTDOORS
ELEMENTARY—SENIOR	INDIVIDUAL	OR INDOORS

This is another of the push-pull challenge-games dear to many tribes. Two players of about the same weight and height stand chest to chest, each one looking over a shoulder of the other, with both arms outstretched to the sides. A line is marked on the ground about 2 long paces behind each player.

When the chief who acts as referee calls "Ready!" the two contestants push firmly against each other, with only a slight bend forward and without actually trying to move the other.

On the word "Push!" each one strains against the other and tries to push his opponent backward to the line behind him, while keeping the arms outstretched. The one who succeeds in pushing his rival up to and over the mark is the winner and counts coup. Again, the fairest way to decide the winner is on the three-tries basis.

The winner of each pair contesting takes on the winner of the next pair, and this can continue until the champion is determined.

BOW!

Plains—Northwest Coast

BOYS	2 TO 8 PLAYERS	OUTDOORS
ELEMENTARY—SENIOR	INDIVIDUAL	OR INDOORS

This is another challenge-game of the same category as the one preceding. It required no equipment and, like most games of its type, was played in slightly different ways by various tribes, the games leaders of which devised such games on a trial-and-error basis.

Two players of about the same size and weight face each other at fairly close quarters, left foot advanced in a boxing position, with the right hand on the opponent's chest and the left hand placed on the back of his head. When the chief shouts "Go!" each contestant tries to make his rival bow his head forward, by a slow, sustained pull with the left hand and push with the right hand. No jerking is allowed and the chief disqualifies the player who uses such tactics. This is still another challenge which is best decided on a two-out-of-three-wins basis.

FOOT PULL

Northwest Coast

BOYS	2 TO 8 PLAYERS	OUTDOORS
JUNIOR—SENIOR	INDIVIDUAL—TEAM	OR INDOORS

This amusing challenge-game provided the Indians, who had a fine sense of humor, with a good opportunity to pull each other's legs.

The contestants sat face to face in pairs on smooth ground, with legs stretched out and slightly apart. One foot of each contestant just touched his opponent's knee. When a chief said "Ready!" each man seized the ankle of his rival's near leg. When the chief shouted "Pull!" each contestant exerted a strong, steady pull in an endeavor to pull his opponent's feet *along the floor* until they were in line with his own waist, without slipping forward himself, for this would aid his rival. Many merry contestants owed their defeat to lusty laughter rather than the strength and skill of their opponents.

Modern Indians contesting this challenge must be very careful to avoid the natural impulse to raise the opponent's leg when giving the first hard tug, since this could cause the opponent to strike his head forcibly on the floor. The leg being pulled must *not* be raised from the ground at any time during the challenge. The best result in three tries will usually establish the winner.

This challenge may also be carried out as a team challenge with the three to four players on each team sitting alongside each other in a straight line, in the manner described, opposite their rivals. There should be a space of about 4 feet between the challengers seated in each line. The winning team is the one which drags the greatest number of opponents forward, as described above in the individual challenge.

The chief staging this challenge must see that it is contested on perfectly smooth ground, so that a contestant has no place to brace either the leg being pulled or the other one.

An old Tlingit shaman informed the writer that he believed this amusing game was a "gift" from their Eskimo neighbors to the north, who contested it sitting on the ice. A comparatively short time ago, along the vast expanse of the Northwest Pacific Coast, a prized gift often took the form of a song, or a dance, or a game! Many of the games in this book are gifts, coming directly from the Indians of the Northwest Coast to their paleface brothers who read this book because they enjoy playing games as the Indians did.

TROPHY SNATCH*

Northwest Coast

BOYS	2 TO 12 PLAYERS	OUTDOORS
ELEMENTARY—SENIOR	INDIVIDUAL—TEAM	OR INDOORS

This challenge-game is best played in a circle measuring about 40 or 50 feet in diameter when there are more than six contestants. Each player wears a 3-inch-wide band of colored crepe paper tied once around his left arm, just above the elbow. The two ends, which should each be 2 inches long, hang down from the reef knot with which the strip is best tied.

The players, by twos, face each other anywhere inside the circle in order to start the challenge. When the chief shouts "Attack!" each pair of contestants either stalk or rush each other in an effort to snatch the opponent's armband. Once this man-to-man attack begins, each pair may dodge about in any part of the circle, interfering as little as possible with the other contestants while doing so. The challengers must not catch, hold, push, nor strike each other, though they may ward off an opponent's attempts to snatch the armband by sparring and using the arms as shields. The attackers may crouch, feint, jump, or try to secure a rival's armband in any fair and not over-rough way. When any two challengers succeed in snatching the bands at the same instant, which happens fairly frequently, the result is counted as a tie.

Teams of two to six can contest one against the other. Each team should wear armbands of a different color. The snatching may be carried out in a chief-supervised free-for-all, by each team starting from different sides of the circle, without pairing off for the snatch.

LOG CHIEF*

Woodland—Northwest Coast

BOYS	2 TO 10 PLAYERS	OUTDOORS
JUNIOR—SENIOR	INDIVIDUAL	OR INDOORS

This was a game played by Indian boys of all ages and many tribes. In this challenge, as in so many others, the contestants drew on Mother Nature's supply for the necessary equipment. It required only a sound, fallen log about 12 feet long and from 8 to 12 inches in diameter, and a stout stick for each player, measuring about 18 inches in length and 2 or 3 inches in diameter. The stick was usually green in order that it would not snap and injure a player.

Usually two challengers started, one from each end of the chosen log, so that they met exactly in the middle of the log. Each player advanced slowly with his stick held by one hand toward the end. It was held slightly in front of him, ready to push hard, but steadily, on the stick of his opponent. As the sticks met and the two players pushed, each taking care that his opponent's stick did not press against his fingers, one challenger was forced to back up after a few moments of pressure. The one lost out who was forced off the log first, either by being forced along and off the end of the log, or who lost his balance and was forced to step from the log. Generally this contest was settled on a score resulting from three tries in succession.

A modern adaptation of this game, which can be played indoors or out, is contested in this way. A stout plank about 10 or 12 feet long and approximately 9 inches wide can be used for the log. It can be laid flat on the floor, which assures complete guarantee against breakage when the plank used is thin; but it is more fun if the plank is thick enough, about 2½ or 3 inches when the plank is a hardwood one, to be supported on two strong wooden boxes or wooden blocks about 12 or 18 inches high. The sticks required for each challenger can be sawed from a stout pole about 2 or 3 inches thick, and the leader must take great care to see that each stick is more than sufficiently strong so that it cannot possibly break when in use.

These sticks must never be struck against each other and a contestant not using steady pressure is disqualified. Contests may start from the middle of the "log."

LANCE CHIEF

Plains—Northwest Coast

BOYS	2 TO 10 PLAYERS	OUTDOORS
ELEMENTARY—SENIOR	INDIVIDUAL	OR INDOORS

Indian boys played this challenge-game testing hand dexterity and speed with a long pole when they could not get hold of a lance shaft or harpoon pole. The pole used can be 8 feet long and about ¾ inch in diameter, with a ½-inch-wide stripe painted around the exact center of the pole. The two challengers face each other, holding the pole in front of them at about eye level. Each challenger holds the pole with his right hand at the extreme end; his left hand grasps the pole and touches his right hand. When the chief says "Go!" each contestant instantly moves his right hand rapidly over his left hand and grasps the pole, with his right hand touching the left hand for a second. Immediately he races his left hand over his right hand to take up a new grip alongside and touching the right hand. These movements are rapidly continued, in the correct sequence, each hand advancing as swiftly as possible toward the mark on the center of the pole. The challenger whose hand first touches the paint stripe at the center of the pole counts coup and wins, provided his hands have moved correctly along the pole and have touched, side by side, for a fleeting moment while making each hand shift.

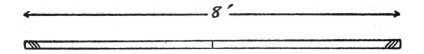

The chief should watch closely to see that each challenger advances correctly on *each* hand shift. If this is not done, a challenger may win unfairly, in the heat of contest and speed of movements, by advancing a hand without touching the other while moving it forward toward the pole's center mark. Any challenger who relaxes his hold with *both* hands for any reason is disqualified. This challenge may be contested on the best-out-of-three-tries basis.

For older challengers who exhibit unusual speed and dexterity in making the hand shifts, the chief may double the hand-race distance. He does this by having them race to the center of the lance and back again to the ends, reversing the hand movements on the return. The challenger whose hand reaches the end of the pole first wins, provided he has observed the hand-touch rules at each shift.

CATAMOUNT*

Northwest Coast

BOYS	2 TO 8 PLAYERS	OUTDOORS
ELEMENTARY—JUNIOR	INDIVIDUAL	OR INDOORS

The idea for this challenge-game came to the author as he watched two Canadian Northwest Coast Indian boys push and strive to shove each other from a narrow tree trunk which lay across two big logs in a forest clearing. Though they contested with no holds barred, the following version has been modified so that it is more tricky and difficult for modern Indians to contest.

A 2 by 4 inch plank, at least 6 feet long, is held firmly in place with the 2-inch side uppermost, by driving two strong stakes securely into the ground on each side and at both ends of the 2 by 4. The two contestants stand facing each other on about the middle of the 2-inch strip. This is done by each standing with one foot advanced in front of the other, the toe of the rear foot barely touching the heel of the foot in front. There should be a space of about 2 feet between the contestants. The right hand of each challenger is advanced slightly, ready for action when the chief gives the command. When he says "Attack!" each contestant, without advancing, tries to force his opponent to lose balance by slapping him on the palm of the outstretched right hand. When a contestant is forced to put even a toe on the ground he loses that bout. This challenge-game, like many others, is best judged on a two-wins-out-of-three basis. The winner meets new contestants until he is defeated, so the last challenger on the strip counts grand coup and becomes champion.

Quite often these contests last far longer than the rather insecure foothold seems to warrant, and it is an amusing sight to see first one contestant, then the other, lose balance, regain it, when such a feat appears to be impossible, and continue the bout. The two opponents striking at each other have the appearance of two catamounts sparring, which gives the challenge its name. Modern chiefs can experiment with this challenge; for instance, letting the opponents spar with the left hands only or with both hands, only the palms of the hands being struck and used throughout the challenge.

TRAPPED!

Northwest Coast

BOYS	2 TO 8 PLAYERS	OUTDOORS
ELEMENTARY—SENIOR	INDIVIDUAL	OR INDOORS

This challenge-game is of a similar type to the one preceding. It is played by various tribes in different parts of the Americas, but because the writer was introduced to it on the Canadian Northwest Coast it is listed as a game played in that vast territory. Perhaps credit should really go to the Eskimo, for an old Tlingit chief said that they got this game, along with others, from the Eskimo people to their north. The Eskimo were a merry, game-loving people who played a great number of games of many sorts, not forgetting challenge and general athletic ones, so it is quite likely that a considerable number of their games were adopted, and adapted, by their nearest neighbors and spread from there to other tribes. This foot-pull game was played in the following way.

Two players of about equal weight went down on their hands and knees facing away from each other with the soles of the feet touching. A piece of strong rawhide about 30 inches long and 1½ inches wide was tied together at the two ends to make a loop. One end of the loop was fastened around the right foot of each challenger, so that it covered the ankle. On the word "Pull!" each contestant tried to drag the other backward for a few feet or more to decide who was the winner. As in the former pull-game, this contest is best played on a

243

two-wins-out-of-three basis. Sometimes four or five pairs competed at the same time, all pulling on the command "Pull!" The champion was found by having the winner of each pair of pullers compete against another winner until the final three pulls established the champion. As in all such games, chiefs and players devised variations, such as pulling with the left foot, and *both* feet, which increased the difficulty for the contestants and added to the amusement of the onlookers.

COPPERHEAD
Woodland—Plains

BOYS   3 TO 6 PLAYERS   OUTDOORS
ELEMENTARY—JUNIOR   INDIVIDUAL   OR INDOORS

In this challenge-game, a keen-eared player was chosen as the "copperhead." Before the game began, a "fang" was made from three or four very light, straight willow branches each about 30 inches long. These were tied together, wrapped around with grass, and then tightly covered with buckskin or lightweight cloth to form a "fang." The copperhead was blindfolded, with ears left uncovered, and sat cross-legged on the ground. The other players, two to six, stood on different sides of the copperhead at a distance of 12 feet. Their positions were unknown to the snake.

When modern Indians play the game, the chief calls "Attack!" and the attackers advance, one by one, in the order in which they are pointed at by the chief. The attacker may walk on tiptoes fairly slowly, or creep, but must not rush the copperhead. The attacker tries to touch the copperhead on the top of the head without being "bitten" by the fang before he can do so. The copperhead must wait until he really believes he hears an attacker close to him before he "strikes." When he does so, he must strike only once and only in one direction—the one in which he thinks he hears sound. The snake must not strike with a circular swoop. If his fang touches the attacker anywhere, that attacker is out of the game; but if he does not touch the attacker, he must draw his fang back to the striking position instantly and wait for the next chance to strike.

The chief in charge of the game may decide that the copperhead cannot be approached directly from behind, as it is more difficult for him to strike in that direction, but usually an attack from any quarter is allowed. The first attacker who touches the copperhead on the top of the head counts coup and may take the place of the snake when that particular challenge is ended. All of the attackers in one challenge are given the chance to go into action, whether the copperhead is touched by an earlier challenger or not. Should the snake be able to strike all of the attackers, he counts grand coup and may, if he wishes, play the role of copperhead again in the next round.

STRONG BADGER
Plains—Woodland—Northwest Coast

BOYS	2 TO 8 PLAYERS	OUTDOORS
ELEMENTARY—SENIOR	INDIVIDUAL	OR INDOORS

Challenge-games of this sort were played by many tribes and in a somewhat different manner in various parts of the country. Here is one way to carry out this challenge which follows the original Indian pattern. Two challengers of about the same weight face each other on hands and knees, with a line marked on the ground between them. A strip of strong cloth or webbing, 60 inches long and about 3 inches wide, is sewn strongly together at the ends. This band is placed over the heads of the two challengers so that it fits comfortably just below the ears. When the center of this band is directly above the mark or stick on the ground, the chief who acts as referee says "Get ready!" and the two players take the strain, to make certain that the headband is correctly adjusted and comfortable. They get ready for the pull by holding the band taut, but do not actually pull at this point.

The chief then shouts "Pull!" and each contestant backs away on hands and knees in an effort to pull the other player over the mark. The one who does so counts coup and wins. The chief may let the winning player pull the loser several feet over the mark so that there is no doubt as to who won the challenge. A player who loses his headband accidentally, or lowers his head so that the band slips off, may be disqualified either on the first or second time it happens. The fairest way to judge the winner of this contest is on a best-out-of-three-wins basis.

The winner of each contest can compete against the other winners in order to decide the champion Strong Badger. When different tribes or groups are competing, teams of four or six badgers each may be formed to decide the winning team.

POLE PULL

Plains—Woodland—Northwest Coast

BOYS	4 TO 12 PLAYERS	OUTDOORS
ELEMENTARY—SENIOR	INDIVIDUAL	OR INDOORS

This individual tug-of-war form of challenge is used by many Indian tribes to develop strong arm and shoulder muscles. All that is required for this challenge-game is a strong straight pole about 9 feet long and 1 or 1½ inches in diameter. A small streamer of buckskin or colored cloth, not more than 1 inch wide, is fastened exactly to the middle of the pole so that it hangs downward. The chief marks a line on the ground behind which one of the two contestants stands; directly opposite that line, at a distance of 7 feet, he draws another line, behind which the second challenger stands, facing his opponent. Exactly halfway between these two lines, the chief either marks another line on the ground or lays a straight stick as a marker between the two contestants. Each challenger holds one end of the 9-foot pole with both hands.

On the word "Pull!" each contestant tries to pull his opponent toward him by pulling on the pole, trying to bring it toward him, hand over hand, without twisting the pole or moving from his original position. The pole should be held just above waist level and can pass on either side of the body as it is pulled in. The player who first pulls his rival over the center line counts coup, though the chief may decide that a player must be pulled right up to within a foot or two of his rival's position. Usually this challenge is best decided on a two-out-of-three-wins basis.

POLE PUSH

Plains—Woodland—Northwest Coast

BOYS	4 TO 12 PLAYERS	OUTDOORS
ELEMENTARY—SENIOR	INDIVIDUAL	OR INDOORS

This challenge is contested in exactly the opposite way from the preceding one. The same pole is required but the contestants push instead of pull. The players stand in the same positions as in Pole Pull but instead of marking a line on the ground between the two challengers, the chief marks a line 3 feet behind each contestant. Throughout the entire challenge the blunt ends of the lance must always be kept on either side of the contestants' bodies, never pointing directly toward their stomachs. On the command "Push!" each challenger tries to advance the lance in a straight line, following up his attack until his opponent is forced back over the line marked behind him. This challenge is, like many others, best decided in the two-out-of-three-wins manner.

SLIP STICK

Northwest Coast

BOYS	4 TO 8 PLAYERS	OUTDOORS
ELEMENTARY—SENIOR	INDIVIDUAL	OR INDOORS

This challenge-game was contested by the boys and men of some of the Northwest Coast tribes. It required a strong wrist and fingers, along with some strength, but a little know-how helped a good deal. Each two challengers needed a round, entirely smooth stick about 18 inches long and 1½ to 2 inches in diameter. The stick was smoothed so that there were no splinters to injure the hands of the players. Once they had secured the right sort of stick, they used whale blubber and other fats to make the slip stick really slippery, but modern chiefs can

248

rub the stick with talcum powder, after it has been sand-papered smooth. The game can be contested within a 12-foot square or circle when there are only two challengers; when there are more, the contesting space can be increased to as much as 30 feet square.

When two contestants of about the same size and weight stand ready within the marked-off space, a chief tells the contestants which hand can be used, left *or* right, then throws the stick straight up into the air, calling out "Go!" as he does so. The challengers then rush to catch the stick as it falls, or when it has reached the ground, and each one tries to snatch it from the hand which first succeeded in securing it. The chief must see that the stick is *never* held above chest level at any time during the contest and that only *one* hand, the one chosen before the bout began, is used throughout the contest. The chief must also see that the hand which is not on the stick is not used in any way and that the contest does not become a wrestling match. The player holding the stick after the chief has counted to 60 or 100, or more, counts coup and wins. In this version, when only two contestants take part, each challenger may be given one end of the stick and the pulling commences on the word "Go!"

When anywhere from three to six players contest with only one slip stick, the challenge becomes more of a rough-and-tumble and it takes a couple of alert chiefs to referee the bout. Such a contest can be carried out safely, however, and provides more fun and excitement for the onlookers, especially when the challengers represent rival teams. The safety rule that the stick must never be held above chest level should be strictly enforced at all times during the contest.

CLATAWA!

Northwest Coast

BOYS   2 TO 6 PLAYERS   OUTDOORS
                           INDIVIDUAL   OR INDOORS

In Chinook jargon the title for this challenge means "Go Away!" Indian boys carried out this challenge with wooden shields made to represent the "coppers" of that region. Indians of the Guiana contested it with real shields. The method of contesting was similar in both cases. The challenge can be carried out by modern Indians who take the trouble to make the simple shield, which can be used time and again for further contests.

The shield can be made from strong, unbending sheets of wood or plywood, 30 inches long, 18 inches wide at the top and about 10 inches wide at the bottom. The wood can be about ¾-inch thick, or a little thinner, according to the strength of the wood used. This shield should be cut into the usual copper shape, as illustrated, and the front of each shield can be decorated with some simple Northwest Coast Indian design. One shield is required for each two contestants.

The challenge can be carried out in a circle, measuring about 30 feet in diameter, or with each contestant standing just behind a line marked on the ground, facing the other. These two lines are exactly opposite each other and 30 feet apart. A third line is drawn halfway between the two lines. When the chief shouts "Ready!" each challenger advances to the center line and the chief gives them the shield. The contestants, facing each other, grasp the sides of the shield firmly, about the middle, taking care that the fingers do not overlap. The opponents should be ready for the next command, for when the chief says "Attack!" each challenger tries to force his opponent backward by steadily pushing on the shield and advancing as he pushes. When one challenger pushes the other either out of the circle or over the line behind him, he wins. The shield should not be twisted or moved violently in any way during the contest. The loser is worn down by the steady pressure of his opponent. The Guiana Indians generally used two shields for this contest, each challenger pressing his shield against that of his opponent.

12.

Ceremonial Games

PAGEANTRY AND CEREMONY had an extremely important place in the games of all Indian tribes of the Americas. Ceremonial dress ranged from magnificent full regalia to the addition of only a sash or scarf to be worn by referees and players. This was only a part of their gala events. Frequently elaborate ceremonies connected with the sun, moon, stars, seasons, and gods were performed by medicine men and chiefs before many of the games could be started.

Certain times and seasons were strictly observed for the playing of many games. They were determined by the planting and harvesting of corn, the drying of salmon, phases of the moon, and many other things governed by nature, natural phenomena, signs and omens.

Any game could be opened and conducted with ceremony when the Council of Chiefs so decided. At least fifty games in this book could have been included in this chapter, but they are better fitted into the various categories in which they are set down. While only six so-called ceremonial games follow, they have been selected to illustrate the fact that ceremony was a part not only of games of chance but also of games of skill, team games, challenge-games, and many others. Ceremony was a part of the actual staging of the games, but it played an important part as well in the sending of invitations to the games and the challenges sent to rival tribes and teams. When, for example, the intrepid Pima runners carried a ceremonial message challenging a neighboring tribe to a relay race, the challenge-invitation ended with a picturesque phrase, such as, "Meanwhile, we are singing the humming bird song and dancing in preparation." The Cheyenne and other Plains tribes opened their Hand Game with a prayer by the chief who was in charge of the games. Some tribes broke into a dance after one side had counted coup, and the dance was finished before another game was begun.

Chiefs of modern Indian bands can, by the use of imagination and a little extra effort, make effective use of the pageantry and picturesque and colorful ceremonies connected with American Indian games. This ceremonial display can be used to great advantage on special occasions, such as Parents' Day, Indian Day, Field Days and Game Rallies.

Little expense is necessary, nor special equipment required, in order to add color and effect to many of the games recorded in this book, as they can be introduced with ceremony and played ceremoniously. This is easily accomplished by the use of some pageantry, an entry march of the players or contestants, a series of rhythmic movements or dance steps by a preselected group, the ceremonial distribution of even simple equipment by a chief prior to the start of a game, the ceremonial placing of a mat or blanket, the use of a tom-tom, beating board, or drum and singing or humming. The ceremonious carrying of a ball to the North, South, East, and West by a chief before a game begins is one of the many simple yet effective ways to introduce a picturesque note into the proceedings.

FIND THE CHIEF
Northwest Coast—Plains

| BOYS OR GIRLS | 7 TO 19 PLAYERS | OUTDOORS |
| JUNIOR—SENIOR | TEAM | OR INDOORS |

To play this guessing game, a great favorite with many tribes, some simple equipment is required. A mat or blanket; another small mat; twenty tally sticks; a plank, sometimes called a beating board, to serve as a drum; four drumsticks and nine wooden disks about 2½ inches in diameter—these comprise the equipment. All necessary information about tally sticks will be found in the introduction to "Guessing Games." Modern Indians can replace the wooden disks with stout cardboard ones of the same size. The disks must always be an uneven number: five, seven, or nine. Whatever the number, all but one are colored exactly alike, blue or yellow being the usual colors, with segments of circles and grouping of dots on each. Some of the Indian painters who made and painted these disks were credited with being able to paint them with magic designs which helped their owners to win. Modern Indians do not need to paint either parts of circles or dots on the disks. The odd disk was the important one; it was colored in brown and red and known as "The Chief." Though the Indians of the Northwest Coast used shredded cedar bark in which to hide their disks, modern Indians whose villages lie far from the Pacific may use a bunch of fine shavings, excelsior, straw, or finely shredded paper in which to hide the disks.

To play this game, an uneven number of players was required. One player was chosen or drawn by lot to hide The Chief. The remaining players who were to guess where The Chief was hidden drew lots to determine on which side they were to play. One team of guessers sat on the North side and the other team on the South side of the mat or blanket. The mat was laid running East and West. About a foot away from it, and toward the Northwest, the smaller mat was spread out and the twenty tally sticks were placed on it. In line with the small mat, to the Northwest, the plank was placed on the ground and the drummers and singers sat around it. The shavings or other materials used in hiding the disks were placed together with the nine disks on the western end of the mat. The hider of the disks sat in front of them. A messenger stood at the eastern end of the mat, facing the player who hid the disks.

Modern Indians can play this game in the same way. The player chosen to hide the disks should be a good actor with dramatic power and the ability to follow the rhythm of the drumbeat and singing. When the players are seated in position, four drummers sit beside the plank-drum, beating out a rhythm and singing a rather monotonous song which consists chiefly of syllables, such as *Eh ya ha eh yah*, repeated over and over again. In the meantime, the hider of the disks spreads the bundle of straw flat on the mat, making a sort of little blanket of it, and places the 9 disks under it. As he works, he makes magic passes over the straw-covered disks, so that The Chief will be well hidden and the guessers puzzled. After moving the disks about under the straw, being careful to keep them well covered at all times, he divides the straw into two bundles, with half of the disks in each. He continues to make dramatic gestures and shuffles the two piles around until a player points to one of the piles. This ends all guessing for that round.

Instantly, the hider of disks stops his movements and rolls all of the disks in the pile pointed to, one by one, to the messenger who examines each disk to see if The Chief is among them. If he finds The Chief disk, he holds it up and all of the players on the side which made the correct guess give a loud shout of victory. At this point the players are in a frenzy, in striking comparison to the hider of the disk, who is completely calm. Following the victory shout, the messenger takes a tally stick from the small mat and sticks it into the ground in front of the successful guesser. If the guesser is wrong, his side forfeits a point and the messenger thrusts the tally stick into the ground at one end of the row of players on the rival side. The disks are then rolled back by the messenger to the hider who shuffles and divides the pile, and the guessing begins again. Modern Indians playing this game toss to decide which team guesses first, and only one player on the team is allowed to point after the team has decided which pile hides The Chief. Before the game begins, modern Indians either decide to take turn about at guessing or allow the side which guesses correctly to continue guessing until it misses.

In the Indian method of play, when a correct guess was made by a player whose side had just lost a point and all the tally sticks had been used, the messenger took the tally stick from the end of the row on the rival's side and stuck it in the ground in front of the successful guesser. One side had to have all twenty tally sticks to win the game, so the tally sticks went back and forth between the two sides until one side had all twenty. Although the Indians played this game patiently for hours on end, modern Indians can stop at any time and the chief in charge can tell which team is leading by counting the tally sticks, and that group counts coup.

STRAIGHT PATH BALL

Plains—Woodland—Northwest Coast—Southwest

BOYS	20 PLAYERS	OUTDOORS
JUNIOR—SENIOR	TEAM	

Shinny was played by at least sixty-five tribes in some form or another all over the Americas. The Haida played this game on the fog-shrouded Queen Charlotte Islands, and their not too far distant neighbors, the Makah, played a form of shinny after they had caught and killed a whale. The whale furnished an important part of the equipment for the game, as a ball was made from one of its soft bones. While shinny was played chiefly by men, Menomini women played this game skillfully on a field several hundred yards long. They, like a number of other tribes, used a single post, one set up at each end of the field, as a goal, while other tribes, especially those of the Plains, used a regular goal, often with a crossbar. As a book could be written on this game and the ceremonies connected with it, perhaps it is best only to describe how it was played by the Omaha and the picturesque ceremony in honor of The Four Winds that preceded their game, which they called *Ta-be.*

Modern Indians can dispense with some of the ceremonial dress, but it is not difficult to provide armbands, red for the East team and yellow for the West team. There were ten players on each team, including Guardians of the Goals. A small streamer of cloth is attached to each goal post; red is flown from the eastern end goal and yellow from the goal of the team of the West.

The equipment used by these Indians for the game included four goal posts made from saplings about 7 feet long and 3 inches in diameter; and another sapling, about 6 feet long and 2 or 3 inches in diameter, to be tied across the goal posts, 1 foot from the top, as illustrated. This crossbar was needed for each goal. The goal posts were driven into the ground, with 4 feet of each sapling above ground. The two goals are set 120 feet apart and directly opposite each other, one goal being set up in the East and the other in the West. The Indians made a ball 3 to 4 inches in diameter from the root of a grapevine, or they used a hair-stuffed buckskin-covered ball. A shinny stick, curved slightly at one end as illustrated in the drawing, rang-

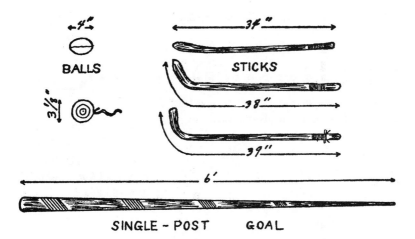

BALLS   STICKS

SINGLE - POST   GOAL

ing in length from 36 to 39 inches, was needed for each player. This completed the playing gear. Each shinny stick bore the mark of its owner so that it could be easily identified. These marks were cut, burned, or painted onto the sticks and each owner's mark was different.

This is how the Omaha chose sides. The chief who refereed the game sat inside the circle in the center of the field, as shown in the following drawing. He was blindfolded and faced North. All of the sticks of the players were placed in a heap in front of him. He picked up the first two sticks he felt, one stick with his left hand and the other with the right hand. He placed the stick picked up with his right hand on his left side and that picked up with his left hand on his right side. He continued to do this until all the sticks were in two piles, one on the East side and the other on the West side. The players ran to these two piles of shinny sticks as soon as the referee's blindfold was removed. Each player took his own stick. If it was on the East side, he was given a red armband; if the stick was on

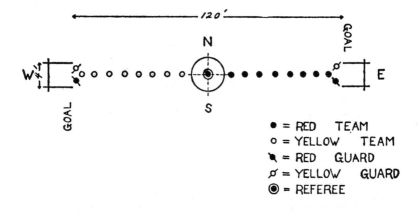

● = RED TEAM
○ = YELLOW TEAM
◥ = RED GUARD
⌀ = YELLOW GUARD
◉ = REFEREE

the West side, he was given a yellow armband. The two teams now formed took up the positions shown in the drawing. There was a guardian from each team at each goal; the job of the Red guard at the Red goal was to try to keep the ball from scoring a goal. The job of the Yellow guard at the Red goal was to help his team drive the ball between the goal posts of that goal. In the course of the game, the guardians at each goal post change their places by a few feet or even yards in order to be in a more strategic position to meet an oncoming ball.

The opening ceremony now takes place. The referee is given a shinny stick and the ball. He lays the ball in the exact center of the circle in the middle of the field and drives it with gentle strokes in a straight path to the North. When the edge of the circle is reached, he picks up the ball and returns it to the middle of the circle. He repeats his former ceremony, this time driving the ball in a straight line toward the South; then, from the center each time, to the West; and finally to the East. The Four Winds thus being honored, the game can begin.

The referee picks up the ball and throws it from the exact center of the circle as high into the air as possible so that it will fall as close as possible to the central point. The players on each side who are nearest to the ball swoop forward and try, with lusty strokes, to drive it toward the rival goal. The ball was usually driven from player to player, though any player was entitled to make a run with it toward the opponent's goal. The efforts of the players were concentrated on making the ball follow as straight a path as possible toward the goal. A ball going over the crossbar did not, of course, score. After each goal scored, the ball was given to the referee who tossed it up, as before, to start the game again. From 4 to 8 goals, scored by either side, decided the winning team. When a goal was scored by either team, all on that side shouted *Ta-be!*

Modern Indians can use a hard or semihard rubber ball from 2½ to 4 inches in diameter, and younger players can get along quite well with a soft rubber ball or tennis ball. The shinny sticks can be made by the players from suitable green saplings, about 1 or 1½ inches in diameter, each decorated with the mark of ownership, cut in the bark or painted or burned onto the stick. The end of the stick should be turned up slightly and tied tightly to the upright part of the stick with string twine or cord until it drys and sets in the desired curve. The drawing shows the best sorts of curves for the stick.

BEAD IN HAND

Plains—Woodland—Northwest Coast

BOYS OR GIRLS	6 TO 12 PLAYERS	INDOORS
JUNIOR—SENIOR	TEAM	OR OUTDOORS

This was one of the most popular of the "games of chance" or guessing games of the Indians of the Americas. It was played, with some variations, by nearly a hundred American Indian tribes. The simple equipment modern Indians need for this game is a pebble about 2 inches long and ½ inch in diameter, or a piece of wood the same size; thirty tally sticks about 12 inches long and ¼ inch in diameter, pointed at one end; a blanket or mat and two planks, about 1 foot wide and ½ or 1 inch thick, of the same length as the mat or folded blanket; and a hardwood drumstick about 14 inches long and ½ inch in diameter for each player.

The blanket or mat is ceremoniously spread out with one end facing the East and the other end the West. The two planks, which serve as long drums, or beating boards, are placed with one on the North side of the mat and the other on the South side. The edge of the mat touches the edge of the beating board. The thirty tall sticks are arranged in two piles, one pile on each end of the mat. The players sit on the ground, one team on the North side of the mat and the rival team on the South side. As a rule, the Indians placed no restrictions on the number of players, the number being decided by how many players could sit comfortably on each side of the blanket. The two rows of players face each other. They draw lots to see which side shall first hold the bead. The leader of the game, usually a chief, always stands behind the row which holds the bead, and the singers, from two to six, stand on the same side. The players on the opposite side of the mat, the guessers, beat time on their drum to the song of the singers. The songs varied among the many different tribes but the gist of the simple song when translated into English runs somewhat as follows: *Ha a ho! Ha a hey ha! Hey a ho! Hi a ho eh! Ha a ho! Ha a hey ha! Hey ho! Hi a ho!—Little bead who holds you hidden?—Ha a ho hey! Ha a hey ho! Ho ho e ha! Ho hey ha!* The players on the other side of the mat beat the time for the singers. While the drummers beat time they also watch the side with the bead very closely as the bead-holding side passes or pretends to pass the bead from hand to hand. Each player pretends to hold the bead, especially when he does not hold it! When any one of the guessers believes he can guess which one of the opposite players holds the bead, he—at any second of the game—instantly points his drumstick at the hand which he believes holds the bead and shouts "Hi!" The hand pointed at must be opened *instantly* the stick is pointed at it. If the bead is in the hand indicated, the chief beside the singers shouts "Coup!" and picks up one of the tally sticks from the guessers' pile and sticks it into the ground in front of the player who guessed correctly. The chief then passes the bead to the successful guesser, gathers up all of the drumsticks and hands them to the other team of players, as the players on that side now do the guessing. The chief and singers change sides, now standing behind the row of players who hold the bead.

When a player guesses incorrectly, the chief takes a tally stick from that side and pushes it into the ground on the successful bead-holding side. The game continues until one of the sides has secured the entire thirty sticks and counts coup! Of course, such a game when played to the very end took, at times, many hours, or an entire day, which is one good reason why a chief in charge of modern Indians may end a game at any point, except when it is a tie, and award the game to the side with the greatest number of tally sticks.

HORSERACE
Southwest

BOYS OR GIRLS	8 TO 16 PLAYERS	OUTDOORS
JUNIOR—SENIOR	INDIVIDUAL	OR INDOORS

This game was known to many tribes in the Southwest territory as Patol House but because these Indians regarded the game as a horserace, with their horses contesting at top speed around the circle, the author has taken the liberty of presenting it to modern Indians under the name of Horserace. It should be noted that this is not a game of chance but one of skill. A good Patol player could almost always throw the number he required by the way he arranged his sticks for a throw and brought them down on the center stone for the rebound. The Keres Indians of New Mexico and other Indians of Sonoro and adjoining tribes used different length sticks and markings on them. The sticks usually measured between 4½ to 7¼ inches in length and from 1 to 1½ inches in width. They ranged from ½ to ¾ inch in thickness and were always made of hardwood. The set of sticks illustrated in the drawing was used by the Tigua of New Mexico and the markings showed how the sticks scored as they fell. Only three sticks were used and they were marked as indicated in the diagram. The "doors" or "rivers" in the Patol House game always faced North, South, East, and West.

This is how modern Indians can play Horserace. The equipment needed is: three hardwood sticks, about 4½ inches long,

1 inch wide, and ½ or ¾ inch thick, marked as shown in the diagram; a smooth flat stone about 6 inches in diameter and either square or circular; and forty stones or circles of wood or cardboard, each about 3 inches in diameter. One stick-marker "horse" is required for each player and a dowel stick 6 inches long and ½ inch in diameter will serve the purpose. The Indians often used a forked twig about 6 inches long. A chief should act as referee.

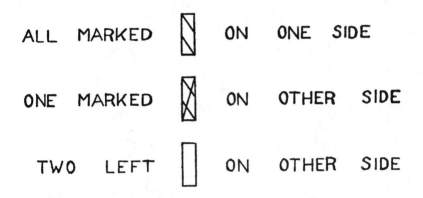

ALL MARKED ON ONE SIDE

ONE MARKED ON OTHER SIDE

TWO LEFT ON OTHER SIDE

The forty stones are placed in a circle about 4 feet in diameter. They touch each other except at the four rivers, which are about 5 inches wide. The flat stone, on which the sticks are bounced, is placed directly in the center of the circle, as shown on the next page. The Indians played with as many players as could be comfortably seated around the circle. The players toss to decide which one will start the game or one may be chosen by the chief. He clutches the three sticks in his right hand, holding them tightly together, either toward the top or bottom, raises his hand level with his chin and then brings the sticks down swiftly and vertically with the lower ends pointing directly at the center stone. When they are about 6 or 7 inches above the stone, he releases his hold so that the end of each of the three sticks strikes the stone and each stick bounces into the circle. The manner in which they fall decides the score. The way to add the points showing on each stick is given in the diagram, page 267. The player uses the river nearest him as the starting point and moves his horse either clockwise, or

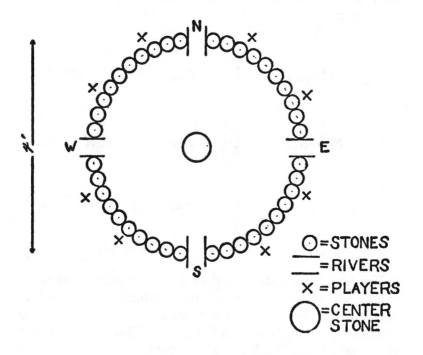

O = STONES
___ = RIVERS
X = PLAYERS
◯ = CENTER STONE

in the opposite direction, around the number of stones which equals the total score indicated by his sticks. If the player throws 3, for example, he places his horse-marker between the third and fourth stones; if he scores 5, he puts his marker between the fifth and sixth stones. If he throws 10, this score will take him into the river and he is given another try. When his second strike takes his horse into any position that counts, and all positions count except the one which lands the horse in the river, the second player either on the right or left is handed the three sticks.

The second player may start from the same river as the first or choose another river, and he may move in the same direction as the first player or in the opposite direction. An interesting checkmate part of the game enters at this point because, if the second player is able to throw the correct number so that his horse lands between the same two stones which the first

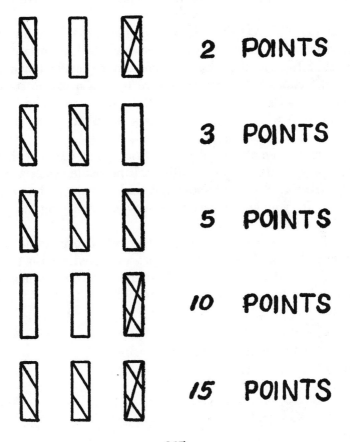

2 POINTS

3 POINTS

5 POINTS

10 POINTS

15 POINTS

player's horse occupies, the horse of the first player is considered dead and the player must take it back to the starting point and await his turn to enter the game again. Only a really clever player chooses to move around the circle in the opposite direction from the player ahead of him, since he will have to try and figure out not only his own moves but those of the players moving in the opposite direction in order to kill horses, while also trying to avoid having his own horse killed. Players' horses may jump over each other without affecting the score, since only two horses landing between the same two stones constitute a kill for the owner of the last horse to arrive in the notch.

The more players there are in the game, the more involved and risky it becomes, for the players have to be constantly on the alert to save their horses from other players moving in both directions. A player may have to return to the starting point a number of times before the game ends. The player counts coup when his horse makes a complete circle and arrives back at its starting point.

Beginners sometimes play this fascinating game with the advance agreement that no kills shall be made. Such a game lacks greatly in interest, however, and is only to be recommended for younger players or those who are playing the game for the first time.

Horserace was frequently played with considerable ceremony and it offers scope to modern chiefs who wish to add pageantry and ceremony. Music is the one thing which was taboo when Indians played Patol House.

HOOP AND LANCE

Plains—Southwest—Northwest Coast—Woodland

BOYS   **2 TO 6 PLAYERS**   **OUTDOORS**

JUNIOR—SENIOR   **INDIVIDUAL**

This game was played throughout the Americas by hundreds of Indian tribes. It was played in a number of ways and with different types and sizes of both lance and hoop. It was frequently called Hoop and Spear and was strictly a warriors' game, never played by women. The Pueblo People used a hoop of woven plants with the ends carefully spliced and the hoop then covered with a strip of leather or woven cloth. Their hoop measured 4 inches in diameter and rolled very well. The spear was 4 feet long and tapered from about 1½ inch at one end to ¾ inch at the other. On either side of this end one half of a barb was fastened, as shown in the diagram. The ends of the barb pointed backward and they had leather teeth fastened inside. A shallow band about 1 inch wide was cut in the other end of the spear shaft, about 18 inches from the end.

PAWNEE

The game was always played from North to South on a level piece of ground from 50 to 100 feet in length. The rival players stood side by side and one player, who had won the right to throw the hoop first, tossed it upward and forward. Both players then ran after it and tried to throw their javelins through it so that the hoop would be caught by the barb and brought to the ground. A hoop caught in the barb counted 1 point, while one caught on the shaft below the band, by a javelin which stopped the hoop and brought it to the ground with the javelin in that position, counted 2 points. Great skill was required to play this game well, not only in throwing the javelin but also in tossing the hoop up so that it offered a poor target for the rival player.

The hoops for this game ranged from 4 to 12 inches in diameter; the Kwakiutl of the Northwest Pacific Coast used a hoop which measured 8½ or 9½ inches. They used a spear 53¼

WICHITA

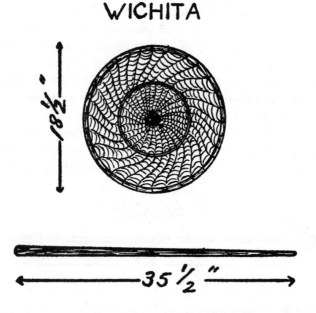

inches long made of partly peeled willow, the ownership mark being denoted by the way the bark was peeled. The general length of spears for Hoop and Lance ranged from 48 to 60 inches, approximately, some of them being of the thickness of fairly stout saplings. This type spear had no barb. The hoop and lance shown in the drawing was used by the Pawnee, while the Omaha and other Plains tribes used similar beautifully constructed equipment. Some Pueblo tribes, among others, used a netted hoop through which darts were thrown by hand or arrows fired from bows. Some tribes played with the hoop in air, others contested as the hoop rolled along the ground.

The easiest form of this game for modern Indians is played as the hoop rolls along the ground. It can be played with this simple equipment. For older players, an ordinary round hoop 6 inches in diameter can be used, while younger players had better use a hoop 12 inches in diameter. The lances can be made from straight pieces of hardwood, or even softwood, about 4½ feet in length and tapering from 1½ inches at the butt to ¾ inches at the thinner end. A stripe 1 inch wide can be painted around the lance 18 inches from the heavy end. The heavy end is pointed forward when the throw is made.

With the equipment in hand the game can be played in this way. Two players stand side by side, one holding the hoop and both being armed with spears held in the ready position. The contestant with the hoop rolls it swiftly along the ground, straight ahead, and both run after it, as close to it as they like, and try to throw a spear through it while it is in motion. Some tribes which played this simple form of the game counted coup when a spear went through the hoop without stopping it; others made it a rule that the spear must stop the hoop and some part of the spear remain inside before coup could be counted. The Woodland Indians often played in this way. As in all other games where even medium-weight objects are thrown, great care should be exercised by the chiefs that this game be played by older boys under strict supervision.

Modern chiefs can introduce any amount of ceremony and pageantry into the presentation of the game.

HAND GAME

Plains—Woodland—Southwest—Northwest Coast

BOYS   8 TO 12 PLAYERS   OUTDOORS

JUNIOR—SENIOR   TEAM   OR INDOORS

This guessing game was played by at least eighty-one Indian tribes throughout the Americas. The term Hand Game replaces one of the many Indian names for the game; it is as descriptive as any of their titles, for it refers to a game in which the guessing concerns objects concealed in one or more hands. Indians generally played Hand Game with from two to twelve men on each side. While many tribes sang regular songs in the opening ceremony and throughout play, "singers" of some tribes simply made a singsong humming noise in order to give the players the beat for their graceful, rhythmic movements of arms, hands, and bodies. This sort of singing is much easier for modern Indians who wish to stage a ceremonial hand game. Here is the equipment needed and the ceremony observed in the playing of a Hand Game by a Plains tribe. Modern Indians can observe as much of the ceremonial part of the game as they wish. First, a flag of one color, about a foot square and fastened to a long stick, is required; also a colorful blanket or rug; three scarves 3 to 4 feet long—one white, one blue, one green; two ceremonial wands 3 feet long and ½ inch in diameter—one with a blue tassel and other blue decorations, the other with a green tassel and green decorations; eight tally sticks with red tassels at one end; two small balls about 1 inch in diameter, or wooden beads of the same size; one drum, or a beating board to take its place; six decorated drumsticks; seven blue and seven green rosettes; four strips of blue paper and four strips of green paper.

A chief in charge of the game places the green and blue strips of paper in a small pouch or covered basket. Each player draws one slip. Those drawing blue slips belong to the North side and those drawing green are on the South side. Each player on the North team is given a blue rosette which is worn on the right shoulder; those on the South team fasten a green rosette on the left shoulder. The flag is raised in the center of a 30-foot circle. The blanket is spread out on the West side of the circle, running lengthwise from North to South. The drum is set in front of the blanket, directly in line with the flag. The blue ceremonial wand is stuck into the ground on the North side of the drum, and the green wand on the South side of the drum. The Keeper, wearing the white scarf tied about his waist, wears no rosette, since he belongs to neither side; he is the one who places all of the paraphernalia mentioned in the correct positions, as shown in the drawing. The eight tally sticks, it will be seen, are placed on the blanket, behind the drum, and run from East to West, lengthwise. The two balls, used for guessing, are placed in front of the tally sticks, at the edge of the blanket. At the end of the game the Keeper gathers up the equipment used and places it in safe keeping.

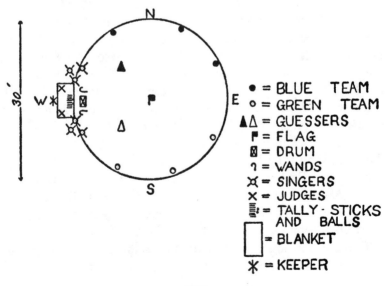

- ● = BLUE TEAM
- ○ = GREEN TEAM
- ▲△ = GUESSERS
- ⌐ = FLAG
- ▨ = DRUM
- ꓨ = WANDS
- ⋈ = SINGERS
- ✕ = JUDGES
- ≣ = TALLY · STICKS AND BALLS
- ▢ = BLANKET
- ✳ = KEEPER

Players on each team choose one of their group to be their Judge. The chief in charge gives the Judge for the North team the blue scarf, and the Judge crosses it over the breast from the rosette on the right shoulder to the waist at the left side and ties it there. The Judge for the South side crosses the green scarf from the left shoulder to the waist at the right side and ties it. The Judges select the six singers, the two guessers, and the Keeper of the equipment, who lays out all equipment, as already described.

The three singers chosen for the North side wear a blue rosette on the right shoulder and sit close to the end of the blanket on the North side. The singers for the South team wear green rosettes on the left shoulder and sit at the South end of the blanket.

When everyone and everything is entirely ready, the Keeper leads the Judges to the blanket where they sit behind their ceremonial wands, the Judge of the North behind the blue wand, on the North, and the Judge for the South behind the green wand. The Keeper then takes the eight tally sticks and divides them equally between the two Judges. As the Keeper picks up the tally sticks, everyone becomes silent. After giving out the sticks the Keeper stands at the edge of the blanket, behind the Judges. The two Judges now rise, the Judge for the North holding his four tally sticks in his right hand and the Judge for the South holding his four sticks in the left hand. They walk side by side to the flag. They face North, advance a few steps, pause, then hold up their tally sticks to the North as all players join in a song hailing the North. At the end of the brief song they lower their hands holding the sticks, walk toward the East, pause, and salute the East with the tally sticks. After saluting the South and West in a similar manner, the Judges return and seat themselves in their original positions on the blanket, laying the sticks between them.

Two guessers are now chosen for a preliminary guessing contest to decide which team will open the actual game. The

Judge of the North calls out the name of one of the onlookers to guess for his side and the person chosen is escorted to his place by the Keeper. The same ceremony takes place when the Judge for the South makes his choice. The Keeper then gives each guesser the wand for his side and one of the small balls. The guesser for the North team holds his hands behind his back, hides the ball in one of them, then holds both hands out in front of him with all fingers closed except the index fingers, which point toward the guesser for the South as he moves his hands in rhythmic time to the drumbeats. When the guesser for the South has made up his mind, he points with his wand to the hand which he believes holds the ball. The hand is opened, palm up, for all to see whether it holds the ball or not. A correct guess counts 1 point. The two guessers take turns, and the first to score 3 points wins the right for his team to open the official game. The Keeper then takes both balls.

The Keeper sets the drum in front of the singers on the side which opens the game. The guesser who wins the right to open the game chooses two players on the team for which he has been chosen as guesser, to hide the two balls. Each takes one ball and conceals it in one hand, then holds both hands out in front of him with the index fingers pointing toward the guesser on the rival team. The two players hiding the balls prearrange secretly between them whether each will hide the ball in the hand nearer his partner or in the hand farther from his partner. One hider must conceal the ball in his right hand and the other hides his in his left hand. Both hiders are free to hide the balls in either hand, provided they arrange to use opposite hands. Since this gives the rival team only two choices, it has a fifty-fifty chance to make a correct guess. As the players hide the balls, all members of their team join in song with their official singers. Then the guesser for the other team points with the wand to the two hands he thinks hold the balls, either the two hands on the outside or the two hands on the inside. The hands are opened so that all may see whether the guess is right or wrong. If the guess is correct, the Judge for that side picks up a tally stick and thrusts it into the ground in front of the team of the successful guesser; but if the guess is wrong, the Judge for the other side credits his team by awarding it one tally stick. To win a sweep, one team has to win all eight tally sticks; and three sweeps by one side decide the winning team.

Whenever a sweep is made, the Keeper is given the two balls and the two Judges rise and go to the flag, each facing in his direction, North or South. The two guessers also go to the flag and one faces East, the other West. All of the players on the winning team form a circle around the flag and sing a short victory song, pantomiming hiding the balls, in time to the drumbeats. After dancing four times around the flag they return to their places.

The Keeper puts the drum on the side of the team which danced the victory dance. The guesser on the opposing side points out the two players who are to hide the balls and the game continues as before. When a team fails three times to outwit the guesser on the rival team, the Keeper removes the drum and places it before the singers of the other team. Then the guesser on the rival team tells the Keeper to whom to give the balls. The side with the drum always sings its own song, and when the drum is changed over to the other team because of three wrong guesses, the other side then sings its song.

The Judges, who appear to be continually calm and undisturbed, despite the frenzy of the teams, direct the course of the game and settle all disputes.

This lengthy ceremonial game is set down with the idea of giving modern chiefs some idea of the multiple details and forms observed by the Indians throughout such a game. Of course, such a game can be played by modern Indians without any ceremony whatsoever—though the Indians of yesterday would not have considered such a drastic thing possible.

List of Illustrations

Index

281

Index

Index

A CATALOG OF SELECTED
DOVER BOOKS
IN ALL FIELDS OF INTEREST

A CATALOG OF SELECTED DOVER
BOOKS IN ALL FIELDS OF INTEREST

CONCERNING THE SPIRITUAL IN ART, Wassily Kandinsky. Pioneering work by father of abstract art. Thoughts on color theory, nature of art. Analysis of earlier masters. 12 illustrations. 80pp. of text. 5⅜ × 8½.   23411-8 Pa. $3.95

ANIMALS: 1,419 Copyright-Free Illustrations of Mammals, Birds, Fish, Insects, etc., Jim Harter (ed.). Clear wood engravings present, in extremely lifelike poses, over 1,000 species of animals. One of the most extensive pictorial sourcebooks of its kind. Captions. Index. 284pp. 9 × 12.   23766-4 Pa. $11.95

CELTIC ART: The Methods of Construction, George Bain. Simple geometric techniques for making Celtic interlacements, spirals, Kells-type initials, animals, humans, etc. Over 500 illustrations. 160pp. 9 × 12. (USO)   22923-8 Pa. $9.95

AN ATLAS OF ANATOMY FOR ARTISTS, Fritz Schider. Most thorough reference work on art anatomy in the world. Hundreds of illustrations, including selections from works by Vesalius, Leonardo, Goya, Ingres, Michelangelo, others. 593 illustrations. 192pp. 7⅛ × 10¼.   20241-0 Pa. $8.95

CELTIC HAND STROKE-BY-STROKE (Irish Half-Uncial from "The Book of Kells"): An Arthur Baker Calligraphy Manual, Arthur Baker. Complete guide to creating each letter of the alphabet in distinctive Celtic manner. Covers hand position, strokes, pens, inks, paper, more. Illustrated. 48pp. 8¼ × 11.
24336-2 Pa. $3.95

EASY ORIGAMI, John Montroll. Charming collection of 32 projects (hat, cup, pelican, piano, swan, many more) specially designed for the novice origami hobbyist. Clearly illustrated easy-to-follow instructions insure that even beginning papercrafters will achieve successful results. 48pp. 8¼ × 11.   27298-2 Pa. $2.95

THE COMPLETE BOOK OF BIRDHOUSE CONSTRUCTION FOR WOOD-WORKERS, Scott D. Campbell. Detailed instructions, illustrations, tables. Also data on bird habitat and instinct patterns. Bibliography. 3 tables. 63 illustrations in 15 figures. 48pp. 5¼ × 8½.   24407-5 Pa. $1.95

BLOOMINGDALE'S ILLUSTRATED 1886 CATALOG: Fashions, Dry Goods and Housewares, Bloomingdale Brothers. Famed merchants' extremely rare catalog depicting about 1,700 products: clothing, housewares, firearms, dry goods, jewelry, more. Invaluable for dating, identifying vintage items. Also, copyright-free graphics for artists, designers. Co-published with Henry Ford Museum & Green-field Village. 160pp. 8¼ × 11.   25780-0 Pa. $9.95

HISTORIC COSTUME IN PICTURES, Braun & Schneider. Over 1,450 costumed figures in clearly detailed engravings—from dawn of civilization to end of 19th century. Captions. Many folk costumes. 256pp. 8⅜ × 11¾.   23150-X Pa. $11.95

CATALOG OF DOVER BOOKS

THE INFLUENCE OF SEA POWER UPON HISTORY, 1660–1783, A. T. Mahan. Influential classic of naval history and tactics still used as text in war colleges. First paperback edition. 4 maps. 24 battle plans. 640pp. 5⅜ × 8½.
25509-3 Pa. $12.95

THE STORY OF THE TITANIC AS TOLD BY ITS SURVIVORS, Jack Winocour (ed.). What it was really like. Panic, despair, shocking inefficiency, and a little heroism. More thrilling than any fictional account. 26 illustrations. 320pp. 5⅜ × 8½. 20610-6 Pa. $7.95

FAIRY AND FOLK TALES OF THE IRISH PEASANTRY, William Butler Yeats (ed.). Treasury of 64 tales from the twilight world of Celtic myth and legend: "The Soul Cages," "The Kildare Pooka," "King O'Toole and his Goose," many more. Introduction and Notes by W. B. Yeats. 352pp. 5⅜ × 8½. 26941-8 Pa. $8.95

BUDDHIST MAHAYANA TEXTS, E. B. Cowell and Others (eds.). Superb, accurate translations of basic documents in Mahayana Buddhism, highly important in history of religions. The Buddha-karita of Asvaghosha, Larger Sukhavativyuha, more. 448pp. 5⅜ × 8½. 25552-2 Pa. $9.95

ONE TWO THREE . . . INFINITY: Facts and Speculations of Science, George Gamow. Great physicist's fascinating, readable overview of contemporary science: number theory, relativity, fourth dimension, entropy, genes, atomic structure, much more. 128 illustrations. Index. 352pp. 5⅜ × 8½. 25664-2 Pa. $8.95

ENGINEERING IN HISTORY, Richard Shelton Kirby, et al. Broad, nontechnical survey of history's major technological advances: birth of Greek science, industrial revolution, electricity and applied science, 20th-century automation, much more. 181 illustrations. ". . . excellent . . ."—Isis. Bibliography. vii + 530pp. 5⅜ × 8¼.
26412-2 Pa. $14.95

Prices subject to change without notice.

Available at your book dealer or write for free catalog to Dept. GI, Dover Publications, Inc., 31 East 2nd St., Mineola, N.Y. 11501. Dover publishes more than 500 books each year on science, elementary and advanced mathematics, biology, music, art, literary history, social sciences and other areas.